This study demonstrates how fruitful the relationship between the social sciences and biblical studies can be if sociological method is imaginatively applied to an account of Palestinian society during the first century. It seeks to show how a sociologist, in examining Josephus' account of the struggle for succession within the Herodian household, would set about asking certain questions about Palestinian society as a whole. The author identifies a succession-crisis that affects every level of Palestinian society, which leads him to ask how that crisis may threaten Israel's capacity to reproduce itself from one generation to the next. As an introduction to the peculiar *craft* of sociology, this book will be of great interest to students of antiquity and of the New Testament.

THE DEATH OF HEROD

THE DEATH OF HEROD

An essay in the sociology of religion

RICHARD FENN

Professor of Christianity and Society,
Princeton Theological Seminary

CAMBRIDGE
UNIVERSITY PRESS

Published by the Press Syndicate of the University of Cambridge
The Pitt Building, Trumpington Street, Cambridge CB2 IRP
40 West 20th Street, New York NY 10011-4211, USA
10 Stamford Road, Oakleigh, Victoria 3166, Australia

First published 1992

Printed in Great Britain at the University Press, Cambridge

A catalogue record for this book is available from the British Library

Library of Congress cataloguing in publication data
Fenn, Richard K.
The death of Herod: an essay in the sociology of religion / Richard Fenn.
p.   cm.
Includes bibliographical references.
ISBN 0 521 41482 2. – ISBN 0 521 42502 6 (pbk.)
1. Herod I, King of Judea, 73–4 B.C. – Death and burial.   2. Herod,
House of.   3. Jews – History – 168 B.C. – A.D. – Historiography.
4. Josephus, Flavius.   I. Title.
DS122.3F46   1992
933'.05'092 – dc20   91–36775   CIP

ISBN 0 521 41482 2 hardback
ISBN 0 521 42502 6 paperback

VN

To Eugene Schneider

Contents

Acknowledgments   *page* x

Introduction   1

1   Two methodological viewpoints: the priestly and
    the prophetic   33

2   Description, interpretation, and explanation:
    modes of analysis   55

3   Levels of observation and of analysis: making the
    right choices   81

4   "What is going on here?" The role of the observer
    and the beginnings of theory   110

5   The search for useful concepts: evil and charisma   132

6   The making of a theory   157

Epilogue   182

References   192
Author index   196
Subject index   198
Index of biblical citations   200

Acknowledgments

First I wish to thank Alex Wright, who has fulfilled his duties as an editor with a thoroughness and grace that have benefitted this book enormously. I am also grateful for the comments of several anonymous readers whose suggestions have improved an earlier version.

It is always a sensitive and sometimes a risky enterprise for a sociologist to discuss an area of interest which is not primarily in his or her field, but James Charlesworth at Princeton Theological Seminary has opened the way for me to begin this inquiry and has been a very helpful and resourceful colleague. I am also grateful for the friendship and encouragement I have received from Pat Miller, Clarice Martin, James Moorhead, Thomas Long, and Donald Capps: all colleagues at the Seminary. Jerry Gorham has provided unstinting and excellent secretarial support.

This book is dedicated to Eugene Schneider, my first teacher in sociology. He mediated the field of sociology through the mind and soul of a humanist filled with criticism and wonder.

Readers may note that all but a few of the quotations are from the Loeb Classical Library edition of Josephus. On occasion, where I have been making use of Cornfeld's work on Josephus' *Jewish War*, I have used his translation as well as his commentary. A few words or phrases from Josephus remain without citation; these are from the Whiston edition noted in the references.

Introduction

Historians have long had before them the thesis that the history of Palestine in the first century CE is shaped by two decisive events, the succession crisis following the death of Herod and the resulting civil war half a century later.[1] It is also the case, of course, that there were a number of intervening factors: the political vacuum that followed the death of Herod; a sequence of inept or vicious procurators and governors;[2] and the fraternal rivalry of the Herodians.[3] In this introduction I will note some of the work that has discussed the years between Herod's death

[1] Schürer–Vermes–Millar (Vol. I: 330–335) prefer the terms rebellion and revolt to describe the various armed struggles in Palestine while the succession was being debated in Rome. The extent of the resistance to Roman rule was very strong, extended to Galilee as well as to the area around Jerusalem, and involved Roman soldiers as well as Jews incensed by the actions of the Roman procurator, Sabinus. There were at least two regional pretenders to the throne.

[2] As Schürer–Vermes–Millar 1973 note, the removal of Archelaus (6 CE) led to the direct rule of Judaea and Samaria under Roman prefects or procurators, whose duties included "the command of troops and the exercise of judiciary functions" along with "the administration of financial affairs" (Vol. I: 372). As the troops were drawn from the gentile population, it is inevitable that their actions reflected popular antagonism toward the Jewish population, regardless of the bearing of the particular prefects in question. Schürer–Vermes–Millar give a detailed analysis of the rule of the prefects, their relation to the equestrian order, and the fate of the Jewish population under particular prefects such as Pilate (see Schürer–Vermes–Millar, Vol. I: 357–398). Clearly the most flagrant in his abuse of power to suppress the Jewish population was Pilate (Schürer–Vermes–Millar, Vol. I: 383ff.). Despite the depredations of the worst of the procurators or prefects, Schürer–Vermes–Millar observe that "Within the limits set by the institutions themselves, the Jewish people none the less enjoyed a considerable measure of freedom in home affairs and self-government" (Vol. I: 376).

[3] "The sons of Herod thus plotted and schemed against one another in Rome," as Schürer–Vermes–Millar described the manoeuvring, after the death of Herod, between Archelaus and Antipas, soon to be joined by Philip (Schürer–Vermes–Millar, vol. I: 331). There were further rivalries brought on by the rivalry between Herodias (Antipas' wife) and Philip, once the latter had received a royal title from Caligula (see Schürer–Vermes–Millar Vol. I: 351ff.).

and the civil war, but will not try to weigh the alternative arguments in any sociological balance; that would be possible only in a book that seeks to bring alternative theories to bear on the discussion of various historians regarding this period in Palestinian society.

What I propose to show is how a sociologist might continue the investigation of Palestinian society on the thesis that the death of Herod and the crisis of succession were of paramount importance for the course of Israel's history. The inquiry here, however, is socio-logical. That is, I want to show how an attentive sociologist might raise certain questions about some of the details of Herod's household and regime. By paying attention to certain details, and by following some of the conventions of the sociologist's craft, it should be possible to examine certain aspects of Palestinian society that are less obvious, perhaps, than the distribution of power and wealth and more elusive than overt social conflict between factions and groups.

I propose to investigate the substructure, as it were, and the informal processes of control and resistance that made that society a virtual prison for many, perhaps most, of its citizens, even when they were ostensibly free to walk about and to dispute the interpretation of the Law. The point is to call attention to aspects of social life that not only shaped the experience of people but may also call into question the viability of Palestinian society. In so doing I would hope to show how these aspects of social life, when taken together, suggest a reality sufficiently pervasive to have shaped the religious movements of the period and the texts that we have come to know as the gospels. Sociologists are typically concerned, therefore, with the hang-ing-together-of-things.

Now, when the life of a society goes relatively smoothly, as it did at times under Herod, not all its assumptions, inner tendencies, and tell-tale signs of strain will come to light; on the contrary, what is most decisive in social life is often latent, implicit, or quite forcibly suppressed. That is why it is important to examine a society when it is coming apart, as it were, at the seams. Only then can one discern the separate pieces, their relative strengths and weaknesses, and the ways in which they fit together and pull in opposite directions. Palestine between the death of Herod and the onset of the civil war (66 CE to 73/4 CE) offers precisely this opportunity to observe what at other times might easily have escaped notice.

No description, no interpretation is either disinterested or complete; all such accounts are informed with a sense of what the historian or sociologist thinks is problematical. I take a "problematik" to be a set of interests and concerns: an interest in how societies maintain order, for instance, or a concern with how they reproduce themselves over time despite the tendency of their members to go away and to die, to resist instruction and to have divided loyalties. If sociologists are concerned with the fate of asceticism in modern societies, for instance, they may investigate the degree to which various ethnic groups produce dedicated workers and self-disciplined citizens, or they may examine the rates of deviance, tax evasion, absenteeism from school and workplace, and disenchantment with major institutions and public figures. Other sociologists, concerned with the ability of a social system to reproduce itself, may focus on these same tendencies but for entirely different reasons. If in this book, therefore, I seem to ignore works that have focused on the same aspects, say, of religion in pre-66 CE Palestine, it is partly because of the difference between my "problematik" and theirs. In a later volume, in which I seek to compare various theoretical approaches to the study of Palestinian society in this period, I will draw more heavily on the secondary literature.

This study, like any other, therefore begins with a brief discussion of the author's own interests and concerns, which indeed focus on the problems that all societies have in reproducing themselves. Societal self-reproduction is a problem that presents itself simply because all the members of any society eventually and inevitably die; they also tend to have strong outside interests or even leanings, and they often think for themselves. This is not to be confused with the general problem of order, or with a more specific interest in asking how societies control deviance. Here the concern is with the task of societal self-reproduction.

More specifically, of course, the book focuses on the illuminating moment of succession: the death of one king and the search
for a new one. In the events leading up to such a succession, in
the twilight of an interregnum, and in the accession of a new
king to the throne, societies tend to reveal their latent loyalties
and tensions. It is the moment of "liminality," as Victor Turner
so aptly terms it. When a society begins to have agonizing
doubts about its ability to reproduce itself over time, about its
continuity and very survival, what has been buried in the way of
antagonisms and hopes, fears and affections often comes forcibly
to light. Even an unpopular monarchy still represents the
viability of an entire society. Succession is a problem, therefore,
not only for a particular household but for an entire society: not
for kingships alone, but for a people in its entirety.

Here I will focus on a variety of such observations, but the
central focus will be on the way that language either reflects or
disguises, expresses or distorts social reality. The need for
surveillance and spies in the Herodian regime did not end with
Herod's death; it continued through the civil war, and it will be
part of our inquiry to ask what it was like to live in a regime
founded on stealth and suspicion.

As words depart from deeds, moreover, the promises necessary to enable one generation peacefully to succeed another fail,
as do the rites and ceremonies that are usually relied upon to
forge alliances, cement loyalties, allay fears of treason, and elicit
commitments for the future.[4] Thus our inquiry will also focus on
the way that the generations fought with each other over the
succession. I will also focus, however, on the tensions within a
rising age-set of young males at odds with each other as well as
their elders for the scarce rewards of maturity and the allocation
of both privilege and sacrifice.

Sociologists often begin where social historians end their

---

[4] If the emphasis on speech and language seems more appropriate to Palestinian
Judaism than to Rome, consider this point made by Veyne, that is, that "A senator
was not a man like other men. Whatever he said was public and was supposed to be
believed . . . Public life was ruled by the will of the governing class, and private life by
fear of what the governing class would say" (1987: 174,176). I quote this here to
make the point that authority was grounded in speech that would normally be
effective, that is, as good as a deed.

inquiries. In this book, for instance, my point of departure will be the insight – not a new one, by any means – that the death of Herod was a pivotal moment in the history of first-century Palestine and accelerated the forces that ultimately destroyed Israel in a disastrous rebellion, revolution, and civil war. That there were problems in the succession after Herod's death is amply attested by Josephus and by contemporary historians; a sociologist such as myself, however, may discern in Herod's problems in managing the succession a larger struggle within the society as a whole: a struggle between generations for the scarce rewards of inheritance and authority.

A crisis of succession, I will argue, is not only pivotal in the life of a nation, but may also be revelatory. What that moment reveals, of course, depends partly on the "motes" and the "beams" in the sociologist's eye. In this book I have begun by suggesting that every sociologist brings a set of problems and concerns into any inquiry. Here my interest is in the ability of any society to reproduce itself from one generation to the next. That ability, I will suggest, depends on many factors, one of which is the ability of speech and language to bear the freight of promises and commitments. Language that can elicit and convey the commitment of one generation to fulfill its duties to the past and to the future of a society is essential if that society is to survive the fateful transition between generations. That is why I will focus on various patterns of resistance, subterfuge, rivalry, and sedition within Herod's household on the assumption that these patterns may have been more widespread and therefore critical to the ability of Israel to reproduce itself over time in pre-70 CE Palestine.

A sociologist is likely to see the world from a very different vantage-point, for instance, from that of scholars who already know when the fateful moments in the life of a particular society have occurred. Once convinced that the latter days of Herod the Great reveal what lies beneath the surface of social life, it is easy for a sociologist to jump to the conclusion that such a moment is not only illuminating but also decisive in the course of Israel's later history. Perhaps the civil war did have its causes in the tempestuous succession to the throne of Herod the Great, but to

assume so from the outset would be to commit the familiar
fallacy of thinking that what comes after an event is caused by
that same event.

   Tempting as it is to search for a single cause, I hasten to add
that there were other, equally pervasive sources of conflict that
nourished suspicion in first-century Palestine. The Hasmoneans
two and a half centuries before Herod had been enormously
successful in bringing the Edomites into the kingdom of Judaea;
their forced conversion produced the later anomaly of an
Idumaean by race, Herod, qualifying for the title king of the
Jews by virtue of his religious adherence. The long-term
tendency of the Hasmoneans to be defeated by their successes is
the theme of Perowne's comment about their subsequent
conquest of Galilee. Speaking of the great-grandson of the
Mattathias who had initiated the Judaean revolt, Perowne
observes that:

Aristobulus reigned for one year only, but it was the most fateful reign
in the whole of recorded history. He subdued Galilee, and forced
Judaism on its inhabitants, thus ensuring that every child born of
Galilean parents should henceforth be born into Jewry, including
Jesus of Nazareth. (1956:18)

This is a pointed reminder that the "Jews" belonged to two
systems: the ethnic and the religious/political. So Herod was an
Idumaean by ethnicity but a Jew by religion because of the
conquest of Idumaea by Hyrcanus, just as Jesus was a Galilean
by ethnicity but a Jew by politics and religion because of the
conquest of Galilee by Aristobulus. The threat to the succession
is obvious: that the king of the Jews is simultaneously a member
of two nations, as it were.

   Add to this the fact that Herod was Hellenized by culture, as
well as Idumaean (Arab) by ethnicity and Jewish by religion,
and one can sense some of the sources of paranoia about an
individual's underlying allegiance in Palestine of the period.
Thus Grant argues that the die was cast when Antony made
Herod the king of the Jews and restored a succession that had
been interrupted by the Pompeian conquest:

This conferment of the royal title upon him was a fateful decision, since
it meant the termination of the national Hasmonean dynasty in favor

of an Idumaean house of recent conversion and Arab race. It also
meant that the kingship and high priesthood must become definitively
separated, since Herod lacked even a shred of family qualification for
the priestly office. (1973:66)

These many strains, between ethnicity and religion, between the
peripheries of Idumaea or Galilee and the Judaean center,
between lines of priestly and monarchical descent, between
genders and, I will argue, notably between generations, make it
inevitable that the kingship, so vital to the life of the nation,
should remain troubled and insecure. The more unstable the
kingship, the more likely it was to maintain high levels of official
secrecy along with energetic efforts to pry open the hearts and
minds of possible rivals and enemies; surveillance as well as
secrecy were twins of the Herodian regime. As Michael Grant
observes, virtually no one could avoid surveillance:

Government was . . . suspicious and severe, with the closest attention
paid to security. Public meetings, other than those summoned by the
authorities, were prohibited, and even an informal gathering of very
few persons was regarded with official misgivings. "No meeting of
citizens was allowed," records Josephus, "nor were walking together
or being together allowed, and all their movements were observed."
Inside the cities, and out on the open roads as well, there were hosts of
men spying on any and every social encounter. The huge fortresses
everywhere, with their frightening reputations, provided a further
reminder that caution was desirable. When Herod died, the dungeons
were found to contain a number of long-term prisoners." (1973:122)

(It is interesting to note that, despite these observations of a
police-state at work in every nook and cranny of Jewish society,
Grant concludes that the regime of Herod was not oppressive:
see 1973:172.)

Given that the later prefects and the Herodian princely states
that followed Herod's death were perennially insecure, it is
entirely possible that the level of surveillance remained relatively high after the death of Herod. The New Testament suggests
that there were informers at the gatherings around Jesus, and
Josephus regards the subsequent governors and prefectors as
relatively weak and incompetent: all the more reason for their
reliance on a network of spies and informers. In any event, it is
clear that Herod was not only a man with a divided tempera-

ment but one whose inner conflicts had systemic origins – and long-term consequences – in the world around him.

Even in these rather cursory selections from some of the secondary literature, it is clear that there are two converging streams of analysis. One focuses on the strains between religion and ethnicity, between outsiders and insiders, between priests and the kingship once the royal household could no longer qualify for the priesthood; the other focuses on the conflict between and within each generation. Let me suggest that there is an interaction between these two sets of factors. I mean simply that the strain of living in two overlapping and inter-penetrating social orders (for example, Idumaean and Jewish, Hellenistic and Israelite) increases the likelihood that the generations, naturally in conflict over the rights and timing of the succession to positions of power and authority, will also be torn between ethnic and political loyalties as these are personified in fathers and mothers, uncles and cousins, sons and daughters. Given the overlapping of dual and competing social orders, it is even more likely that each generation will be disloyal to one or the other set of authorities, thus exacerbating the inevitable tensions that accompany the succession of the generations.[5]

Indeed, Herod typified in himself the danger of a rising generation of males in a society that combines conflicting orders of loyalty and adherence, both ethnic and political. Perowne notes, for instance, that Herod could be "quixotically faithful and loyal to a relation or a friend" and yet put members of his own family to death. This strange combination of brutality and fidelity, Perowne goes on to say, "had its origin in his early youth, when the traditional family piety of the Arabs . . . came into conflict with the stark competition for power and survival which alone governed the Roman world during his boyhood, and for some years after it" (1956:46).

---

[5] Schürer–Vermes–Millar note that "The existence, side by side, of a dual organization in the country, Jewish and Roman, each with its own legal system and its own judiciary institutions, occasionally had irregular results . . . Jewish courts decided in accordance with Jewish law. Even in cases of criminal law the same situation almost always prevailed, with the exception, however, of political offences . . . Even Roman citizens were not totally exempt from complying with the requirements of Jewish law" (Vol. I: 377–378).

Conflicts of loyalty or affection appear to have plagued the household of Herod after his marriage to Mariamme in what Perowne calls "fatal nuptials": fatal because the old factions became part of his household (1956:70). Mariamme was a member of the family of Hyrcanus: that is, she was a Hasmonean, and as such she could give ethnic and religious legitimacy to Herod's kingship. Unfortunately for Herod, she did not return his affections but was in fact a fifth-column within his regime: a source of nationalist intrigue and enmity. Eventually Alexandra and Mariamme conspire to get a Hasmonean high priest, Mariamme's popular brother, appointed to the office, and this intensifies Salome's – and other Idumaeans' – hatred for the Hasmoneans (Perowne 1956:73). In the end, it is Queen Alexandra's "fatal schemes" and "corroding ambition" that caused the deaths of the leading male members of the Hasmonean line for their part in her plots to overthrow Herod (1956:77). The country – the house – divided against itself could hardly stand.

It may be that the civil war thus began in the attempt to unite the Idumaean and the Hasmonean factions by marriage, divided as they were by class and status as well as by ethnicity. A similar argument has been made by Lincoln (1989) about the causes of the St. Bartholomew's massacre: that Henry, by forcing a marriage between Catholic and Protestant in his own household, breached ethnic boundaries that the people in turn were all too willing to restore by violence. The Herodian household also failed to unite through marriage and kinship an otherwise divided system. Not only did the attempt fail; the breach became irreconcilable when the Idumaean faction, led by Herod's sister Salome, incriminated Mariamme of infidelity and sedition. Salome's plot worked, and Herod had Mariamme put summarily to death. From then on, Perowne warns us, Herod "became moody, suspicious, and liable to sudden accesses of vindictive passion" (1956:86). Eventually the split between Hasmonean and Idumaean was passed on to the next generation. Herod's son by Mariamme, Aristobulus, married Berenice, one of Salome's daughters by an Arab prince. That gave Salome a chance to carry on her Idumaean vendetta against the Hasmonean line of Mariamme into the next generation, where the succession foundered.

Grant not only attributes the question of the succession to the chronic internecine warfare in Herod's household but credits that familial discord with undermining Herod's reputation among rivals and allies in the Middle East:

> In Herod's heyday, Augustus had granted him the unique privilege of being allowed to make his own choice from among his numerous sons and thus to nominate his own successor. But this privilege at some stage was revoked, and meanwhile his prestige at Rome suffered greatly when Roman governors of Syria, and even Augustus himself, found themselves drawn with increasing frequency into these desperately unsavory disputes. (1973:78)

I do not want to engage in a historical speculation as to whether the Hellenization of Palestine or the crisis in succession following the death of Herod was more important to the eventual outcome. No doubt the pride and the decadence of the Hasmonean side of the Herodian household, through Mariamme and her sons Alexander and Aristobulus, were pitted against the outside influences represented by the Idumaeans: a clear legacy of the Jewish nationalism that earlier had resisted Hellenization under Alexander Jannaeus. Thus Perowne (1956:113) says that Josephus "rightly" traces the fatal rebellion of the first century to the resistance that began against Antiochus Epiphanes over two centuries earlier and continued to disturb Israel under Alexander Jannaeus. Certainly the causal linkages are too long and complex to be disentangled by the relatively simple logic that I will be employing for this inquiry. Besides, in any moment such as the struggle for the Herodian succession, the effect of past events is reflected in contemporary tensions; all the more visibly if previous tensions have never been fully resolved.[6]

In any event, Herod's appointment as king of the Jews

---

[6] It is important to note, for instance, that even movements of cultural defence against Hellenization may have actually continued the process under new auspices; thus Hengel notes that "the Hasmoneans did not really slow down the 'process of Hellenization' in Palestinian Judaism but in fact continued it as soon as they themselves came to power" (1980: 117). It is an observation such as this that makes it difficult for me to trace Palestinian society's difficulties in self-reproduction to outside influences such as Hellenistic culture.

revealed, reflected, and intensified strains in the nation that the kingship was intended to transcend and relieve; those strains became critical, I would argue, at Herod's death. The failure to transcend that crisis meant that various kinds of conflict, initially chronic and more or less fitful, would be continuous and increasingly intense until the most drastic decisions were taken to purify the nation in the events prior to the civil war.

Some of those strains, as Goodman (1987:116–133) points out, were due to the lack of legitimacy in the ruling elite themselves. Deriving their status entirely from their Roman appointment and their connections with Herod, the *nouveaux riches* lacked the only bases of legitimacy that Israel allowed, namely noble birth, wisdom, or expertise in the Torah. As Goodman observes, that expertise was not the privilege of a single class; even the poor could claim it. This egalitarian streak offset the tendency of specialists in the law to monopolize wisdom and disenfranchise the less well-born; the latter could still become skilled in the Torah through attendance at the synagogue.

Despite these historical reflections, however, the sociologist is seeking to work at another level of interpretation: at processes that run concurrently, that are endemic to a society, whether or not they are fateful for its development or eventual demise. That is why I will be focusing on the task of reproducing a society from one generation to the next. To accomplish that task a society must ensure a supply of individuals fit to enter the roles vacated by their elders. To pass on a cultural legacy is only half the battle between the generations: it is also necessary to link the next generation's sources of inspiration to the prior generation's sources of authority.

With these problems in mind, a sociologist will inevitably focus on conflict within and between generations. In using the illustration of fratricide, moreover, I am also suggesting that there may well have been many other households divided within – as well as between – generations, especially among brothers, only one of whom can be the first-born and heir. Consider Perowne's point that "Indeed, Plutarch tells us that among the Seleucids (as afterwards with the Ottomans) it was regarded as a 'mathematical axiom' that on attaining the throne, a king should murder all his brothers. Among the more humane Jews the axiom did not hold; but the consequences had to be faced" (1956:18).

Perowne's is the kind of observation likely to stimulate a sociologist to search for a pattern of rivalry within and between generations that could jeopardize the future of the society itself. Whether or not inter-generational strife and fratricide were common throughout the Middle-East regardless of the religious persuasion of the nation in question, it is crucially important to note whether Israel was being split apart by such conflict in the years between the death of Herod and the civil war of 66–73/4 CE.

Of course, Roman society had at least its fair share of the sedition of the period. The following poem was written about a "vulnerable slave" who could not dare to speak his mind fully even when he saw treachery being honored. The slave in question was named Cordus; he had been punished by his master, Sejanus, for being too outspoken when public honors were being accorded to his dishonest and treacherous master.[7] Later, in fact, that same master was strangled by Tiberius for creating a conspiracy against him among senators, freedmen, and even soldiers. The poem, by Phaedrus, expresses the corruption of language that takes place when outspokenness is rewarded with punishment:

> I shall now tell briefly why the genre of fable
> Was invented. The vulnerable slave
> Dared not speak his mind and so
> Changed his private feelings into fables and
> Evaded calumny by humorous inventions.
> Aesop's track I have made a highway
> And have created additions to his legacy,
> Favoring some additions which brought me calamity.
> Yet if the prosecutor had been one other than Sejanus,
> If the witness another, if indeed the judge had been one
>   other than he,
> I would admit that I deserve troubles so great
> And would not assuage my pain with cures such as these.
>
> (*Fables* 3, prologue 33–44; quoted in Braund 1985:49)

[7] The main sources for this story are Josephus, *Antiquities* XVIII.181–182, and Seneca, *Consolation to Marcia* 22.4–7; see Braund 1985: 47–49.

Note that the poem concludes with allusions to a trial, with a prosecutor unlike Sejanus (and therefore capable of permitting one to say what one means without circumlocutions). As I will show in this book, Josephus, too, looked to the trial as a forum for language to be uttered that is clear and straight in its meaning and intent, but part of the tragedy to which Josephus points is that under Herod no such forum really existed, and speech could not therefore bear the burden of expressing and sustaining promises and commitments. Furthermore, competition within and between generations, just as between slaves and masters, could not be voiced directly, but was communicated subversively through closed networks. This encapsulation of language among the few who could be trusted with the knowledge of one's real motives, intentions, and meaning resulted in a further distortion of speech when outsiders were present and in even further separation of language from social reality. That is why I will examine Josephus as a witness to flaws in the substructure of words and deeds, speech and action, language and reality, performance and commitment: flaws in the nation that could make continuity and succession virtually impossible.

No doubt the chronic suspicion in Herod's realm was reflected in – and intensified by – the rising age-set of young men eager for authority and impatient of existing controls. Furthermore, this suspicion among brothers was not unusual; as Perowne notes, it affected the Romans as well as the Jews and exposed Caesar as well as Herod to danger from thwarted fraternal ambitions. Especially where a man of Herod's superb abilities and swift action is concerned, however, other explanations for his paranoia and self-destruction are called for; Varneda, for instance, argues that "one is bound to attribute the cause to a transcendent force," (1986:85).[8] For Josephus that force may be God, demons, or worse fates, but even Josephus is clearly not thinking sociologically at this point. It was, more-

---

[8] It is not entirely clear why one is so bound (to seek transcendental causes). Tacitus explains imperial paranoia as though it were an occupational disease: incumbent on uneasy incumbents of the throne, so to speak. Of Tiberius at his succession, who appears somewhat nervous before the senate, Tacitus writes: "Afterwards it was understood that Tiberius had pretended to be hesitant for another reason, too, in order to detect what leading men were thinking. Every word, every look he twisted into some criminal significance – and stored them up in his memory" (1956;1988: 36).

over, a rhetorical strategy to appeal to divine intervention as an explanation, especially when one was accused of being up to no good or was threatened with punishment (Varneda 1986:200). References to the fates constituted a pious sort of appeal which Josephus employed primarily for his Hellenistic audiences; when addressing Jews he was much more interested in Herod's fidelity to the law (Cohen 1987:148). Since I am addressing individuals who are wondering whether sociology may offer a method for gaining insight into the social background of the New Testament, of course, I am inevitably far less interested in the fates and in the transgression of the law than in the more proximate social causes of Herod's suspicions and failures.[9] My purpose, however, is not primarily to speculate on factors that may have contributed to a crisis in the life of Israel decades prior to the civil war itself. The point is to show how sociologists, in examining a limited set of observations about a society, may begin to interpret and even to explain what it was like to live under the apparent conditions of the period. If in doing so historians find the discussion useful, this is all to the good.

The rather pedestrian steps in sociological inquiry along which this book is organized have at least the virtue of being completely different from some of the stylistic features of Josephus' historiography. There seems to be no doubt that Josephus, like other authors of the period, took liberties with his sources, allowed his interest in themes to overcome his respect for chronology, and was not only inconsistent but occasionally irresponsible in the recording of details: he was not "a meticulous and attentive craftsman" (Cohen 1987:47). Varneda (1986) speaks at numerous points of Josephus' tendency to exaggerate, to see tragedy as not only lamentable but unprecedented in scope and in horror; Josephus tends to lend drama to events by speeches and by reflecting on the role of transcendent intervention; in the end there is débâcle and battle. To begin a

---

[9] For an extended discussion of how Josephus tailored his interest in the Law and in fate to his various audiences, see Gunther Baumbach, "The Sadducees in Josephus," in Feldman and Hata 1987: 173ff.

sociological inquiry, however, it is necessary to disenchant the universe of the text and to ask rather simply, "What is going on here?"

What preoccupied Josephus' attention may not be the same constellation of events that fills the sociologist's binoculars. One of the pleasures for the sociologist who reads Josephus is his "eye for the avenues of influence, however shady they might be," as Perowne (1956:110) so aptly puts it. Of course, the sociologist will not necessarily focus where Josephus does; there are other "avenues of influence" to be investigated. Rather than ending in some dramatic encounter or conflagration, for instance, the sociologist's more "synchronic" inquiry is likely to end near the place where it begins: somewhere in the middle of things.

None the less, there is a certain similarity between the inquiry proposed here and Josephus' way of writing history. Like Josephus, I wish to give "special attention to certain events which make the situation impinge in the mind of the reader in a surprising manner" (Varneda 1986:163). Those are the events surrounding the trials and eventual executions of three of Herod's sons: those most directly in line for the succession. These events disclose the erosion of discourse, the use of subterfuge, and the divorce of words from deeds: the decay of what underlies social life and makes any society possible.

As for the historians' interest in what in fact caused the eventual dissolution of Israel in civil war, I can only hope that a sociologist's inquiry will not add more confusion to an already complex topic. In one sense, the problem of what caused the civil war in Israel is as intractable as the perennial discussion of the causes of the civil war in the United States during the nineteenth century. There is no "control group," as sociologists would put it, through which to test alternative explanations or speculations on what might have been. Josephus himself, of course, takes a variety of views as to the causes of the Jewish civil war. In *The Jewish War*, he places responsibility on the brigands, but in the *Antiquities* he finds a wider range of targets to blame. While some, like Cohen cited above, argue that this reflects a change in the audience of Josephus, I would like to suggest that this change of blame for the war may well reflect a process of creating scapegoats that is typical of other communities that have suffered disasters.

Especially where the blame for a disaster is not publicly assigned and guilt assuaged in satisfactory tribunals after a disaster, it is not unusual to find the people creating scapegoats of a wide range of individuals, from particular culprits to public officials, the more notable citizens, and even the basic institutions of the community itself. Such a transition to a broader range of scapegoats may well underlie Josephus' argument in the *Antiquities*, which finds not only procurators but also high priests and notable citizens at fault for the destruction of Jerusalem (see Cohen 1987:152ff.). It is difficult – but none the less imperative – to avoid taking these judgments at first as if they supplied ready-made explanations for the sociologist or historian. Instead, these elements of the society, whatever their own limitations and failings, may have been handicapped by the same patterns of inter- (and intra-) generational rivalry that I am proposing to document, with their attendant effects on the corruption of speech and language.

In a society where succession, both in the royal household and among the most ordinary householders, is in question, social credit is at a premium. By "social credit" I mean in part the reservoir of trust extended to those in authority and to public institutions by those who must pay the necessary forms of taxation and tribute to maintain not only the regime but the system as a whole. As Goodman notes, however, "Neither the ciphers trusted by Herod nor the rich new men thrust into positions of importance *faute de mieux* by Roman governors could command the respect and trust of the nation which, according to the Roman view of things, they were expected to lead" (1987:44). In this one telling observation Goodman points to one outcome of the succession crisis in Israel at the death of Herod the Great. It is Goodman's view that a political vacuum existed at Herod's death precisely because Herod had sought to eliminate all countervailing sources of power and prestige in Judaea during his lifetime.

How could Herod have created a vacuum such that no power could fill it with legitimacy or rule effectively? Certainly Herod had killed a number of Pharisees and Sadducees; he had also arranged the murder of the only high priest who could inherit the Hasmoneans' influence with the people and substituted a line of relatively weak and unknown priests in his place.[10] The rivalry among Herod's sons continued after his death, and Goodman (39) argues that it was his brothers' enmity that produced the removal of Archelaus, the first ethnarch of Judaea on Herod's death, ten years later. Thus Herod had made it difficult for the Romans to follow their usual practice of entrusting local rule to notables who enjoyed considerable influence in their own country and who could be counted on to conduct a census and raise taxes from the Roman tributaries without arousing undue opposition.

On the contrary, by design Herod had created a class of new and relatively rich landholders whose only claim to authority was that they enjoyed his favor. The Romans either believed in or were content to perpetuate the fiction that the notables were respected by the people: a "natural" set of leaders. It was a situation that prevailed for over half a century after Herod's death. Even at the time of Josephus immediately before the civil war of 66–70 CE, the rulers were held in relatively low esteem by both the people and the Romans themselves. As Goodman puts it, even the Roman governors "could not bring themselves to see the Jewish ruling class, for all the pretensions they had evolved at least by the time of Josephus, as quite worthy to be treated as an ordinary provincial elite" (1987:46).

No doubt Goodman's thesis is correct, i.e. that an illegitimate and ineffective ruling class, ridden with its own dissensions, could not provide a way of mediating between the province of Judaea and the Roman empire, between the inside and the outside, as it were. Thus the inside of Judaea becomes permeable to outside influences: to pollution that infects the body politic.[11]

---

[10] Cornfeld makes the point exactly: "The nominations to the high priesthood had become the prerogative of Herod the Great . . . This new process of nomination by the king . . . deprived the high priesthood of its value, contrary to previous tradition which regarded the office as a life-appointment" (1982: 110, n. 562(b)).

[11] Again, it is important to separate the *fear* of outside influences from the practices of adopting or resisting Hellenism. Hengel notes that Hellenistic culture was as influential in Palestinian Judaism as in the Diaspora; indeed, "it affected almost all

If concerns for purity were paramount in the years preceding what is now coming to be known as the holocaust of 66–73/4 CE, however, we need to look further than the obvious intrusions, for instance, of Hellenism into Palestinian Judaism, where it had been widely received even among those elements of the population most hostile to "outside influences." As Hengel puts it:

> the opposition too, the Hasidic apocalypticists or the Jewish Hellenistic apologists, all of whom wanted to preserve the ancestral heritage intact, did not escape the influence of the thought of the new age in this intellectual and political struggle. (1980:125)

In this book I wish to investigate some of the other structural factors that made the death of Herod and the resulting crisis in the succession an enduring aspect of social life in the Judaea of the first century. We will investigate the nature of the succession from fathers to sons, and the rivalry not only between generations but within the succeeding generation itself. As Goodman noted, it was the competition among the Herodian brothers that first unseated Archelaus after ten years of rule. That rivalry, I will suggest, had roots and ramifications in the larger society, and its presence in the Herodian household was thus of symbolic as well as strategic importance for the society as a whole.

More is at stake here than the management of social conflict. No doubt Goodman is quite right that Israel reached a crisis just before the civil war: a crisis in which the ruling elites could no longer rule. There were several reasons for that inability, not the least of which was that the elites were still the parvenus that they had been when first installed by Herod to take the place of notables whom he had murdered. In Roman eyes, Goodman argued, they may have had the legitimacy conferred by wealth, but this presumption did not typify Judaean society, in which wisdom rather than wealth was the token of public esteem, and

strata and groups of the population and involved both the political and economic and the intellectual and religious spheres" (1980: 125). In the same passage, however, Hengel goes on to note that even the apologists and apocalypticists among Jewish nationalists were profoundly affected by Hellenistic culture and indeed used it in the defense of Jewish culture and institutions. An analogy might be found in the nationalism of Japanese elites when combined with a strong xenophobia and hostility towards the West.

that token was conferred on the learned rather than the propertied, regardless of their assets. What I am seeking to explore, however, is not the precarious balance between legitimacy and effectiveness in Judaean society, no matter how delicate that balance was and how easily upset by economic decline or inflation. Instead, I am intending to look at the underlying tissues of the body politic, which can only be examined when they are exposed at certain critical moments. The succession is one of those moments, and when the succession does not go smoothly, one can perceive forces and structures that otherwise lie below the surface of social life.

Goodman's thesis, that Judaea was undone by factions in the ruling class itself, underscores the impact of an incomplete succession at the death of Herod. The conflict among families from whom the high priest was to be chosen included individuals who felt that they had a claim to the Herodian succession (Goodman 1987:139–141). Nor was this conflict polite: Goodman reminds us that each member of the elite was able to hire bodyguards and thugs for protection and persuasion. No doubt members of Herod's family formed a major faction in the Judaean elite and apparently enjoyed increasing popularity, even a tenuous sort of legitimacy, in the twenty years prior to the civil war. In this unhappy period after the death of Herod, I would argue, other divisions were also revealed: not only the split between the generations, but fratricidal rivalry within the ascending generation.

Under these conditions speech veils rather than reveals what is happening below the surface. A fatal flaw thus emerges between what is said and what is done, both in private and in public. Herod sought to probe below the surface of social life, both in his household and in the larger society, through inquisition and its attendant terrors; others may have sought to close the gap between what is said and what is actually done by intensifying sacrificial obedience or through extraordinary devotion, whether in solitude or community. What is at stake is not merely the usual popular resentment of an elite, intensified though this may have been by an elite that governed, as Goodman puts it, though "Roman patronage" rather than by "good birth or wisdom through knowledge of the Torah" (1987:132). At issue is the ability of the society to renew itself from one generation to the next and to overcome the real and symbolic sources of disruption and death for the society as a whole.

It is only fair to warn my readers, however, that this book will not be an "introduction" to the sociological study of the New Testament; it is really an introduction to the method of such an inquiry. I have noted that the problem of the succession of the generations is a "problem" only to those with a specific interest, for example, in the management of social conflict or – as in my case – in the ability of a society to reproduce itself and so achieve a measure of continuity. Now, there is no way to investigate such a problem in any detail without a set of questions to be asked; and those questions, of course, stem from one's theoretical orientation. Let me therefore suggest three separate theoretical orientations to illustrate how they give rise to various – and sometimes quite different – sets of questions.

Suppose we begin with what is often called a "structural-functional" orientation: that is all it is, simply a way of looking at life that gives rise to particular questions. Shmuel N. Eisenstadt (1956), for instance, notes that every society must manage the fate of the young if it is not only to survive but pass on its legacy of values and ways of living; the problem is how to do so in a way that also meets the needs of the young for satisfaction, recognition, and achievement without violating the prerogatives of the elders or putting demands on the society that it cannot meet. What Eisenstadt wants to know, then, are the conditions, the social conditions, which make it more or less difficult for a society to achieve this goal.

Specifically, he asks, how much continuity is there between what a family expects of its young and what the society itself requires? How do the age-sets or age-groups into which the young enter on the way to adulthood foster the ideals and train the young in the disciplines and roles of the larger society while giving them some of the solidarity and emotional freedom permitted by the family? To what extent is the opposition between the generations managed by elders from the larger society who act as wardens or guides to the young? How segregated from older groups are the young for the time that they live within specific age-groups? How separate is the kinship system in general from the political or economic systems? These are the sorts of questions, that is, about the structures of a society and how they function, that rise from such a theoretical orientation. To answer such questions, of course, would require a massive account of information about the type of society that one is investigating as well as about its specific institutions like the family.

For instance, in a later work of which Eisenstadt is the editor, A. H. M. Jones (1955; 1967:162) argues that "the peasant freeholder seems to have survived in far greater numbers in the East than in the West." Those freeholders in Palestine, however, were under serious disabilities stemming from tithes, taxes, inflation, and absentee landlordism. These pressures would have disrupted the ability of younger age-sets to inherit the property of their elders in due time, especially when that property was being absorbed into larger holdings by the Roman proprietors. Under these conditions social groups that provided a "holding tank" for age-sets waiting to come into their inheritance would be severely strained in performing such a function. One might even expect to find rebellion on the part of age-sets deprived of their legacy and yet still expected to pay forms of deference and tribute to their elders. Of course this is purely speculative, but it suggests the scope and difficulty of investigations sponsored by structural-functional orientations.

Even if it is out of fashion to be a structural-functionalist, the logic to which that orientation gives rise is still useful: it serves, for one thing, to determine whether one is doing sociology or social history. To look at the world synchronically, to ask how apparently unrelated observations fit together into a social pattern or social conflict: these are the hallmarks of sociological "verstehen."

On the other hand, there is no substitute for the work of social historians who can draw distinctions between the way one society "functions" and another. Take, for example, Goodman's very interesting observation about the Palestinian Jews' attitudes toward youth:

Jews do not seem to have reacted with hostility to precocious youths: whereas the Romans imposed minimum age-limits on holders of magistracies, the Jews did not apparently disqualify young men from the high priesthood; neither Josephus nor the Gospels seem abashed in reporting the juvenile genius of their heroes; and it is striking that inscriptions on Judean ossuaries do not include the age of the deceased even when he is elderly, in contrast to common practice elsewhere. (1987:123–124)

If it were not for social historians like Goodman, this sociologist, at least, would not know that Judaeans provided such opportunities for the young or revered wisdom rather than age. On the other hand, as a sociologist I would want to know the answer to several more questions. Did the priesthood "function" as a way of siphoning off discontent from youth? Did oratory work, as it does in other "traditional" societies, as a way of enabling the rhetorically gifted to compete with their elders and for the society to recruit new leadership regardless of the disadvantages of birth and kinship? Did this relative openness to youthful talent persist even when the high priesthood as an institution was under severe pressure from Herod and from factional disputes? Were there some radical youth who refused to be co-opted by the prospect of high priestly status? Did the offer of priestly status to gifted or outspoken youths work without regard to kinship and social class, or were these latter aspects of social life filters that screened out many of the gifted young, who might then seek other ways to display and to assert their talents? These questions, typical of a structural-functional approach, might – or might not – be asked by a social historian whose interests have been honed to suit a somewhat different orientation.

On the other hand, one could ask questions of a slightly different order if one came at the subject as might a "structuralist." The interest is the same, that is, in how a society can achieve continuity and reproduce itself. The orientation, however, is toward symbols that stand for the dangers and enemies, the sources of rivalry or pollution, that the society in question believes itself to be confronting.

Out of this orientation come a variety of questions about the ways a particular society may confront and conquer in myth or symbol, in rite or drama, the evils that beset it. In studying a myth, for instance, one would ask about whether the young are portrayed as an outside influence, or as strangers and aliens: foreigners who pollute or endanger a society with new and subversive ideas and values. Does the society in question supply youth with what some have called a "liminal" period, a twilight zone between youth and adulthood, in which the young are literally outside the normal structures of a society and thus "outsiders" – or "aliens" for the time being? Are there teachers within a society who in fact compound the danger by teaching new gods to the youth? Are there immigrants or other sources of cultural invasion that bring outside influences to bear on a society and appeal particularly to the youth? Do the rites of a society reflect clear and present or largely imaginary dangers to the symbolic continuity of a particular society? If women did not exist, would a patriarchy invent them? If the young did not exist, would not elders also have to invent a surrogate danger or some other source of rivals or of innovations? As in the case of structural-functionalism, these questions would require a careful investigation and an adequate supply of information; both conditions lie far outside the scope of this book.

Note that the community's ability to maintain and reproduce its spiritual legacy confronts various sources of discontinuity and disruption personified by the uncontrollable or alien elements of social life (exchange, sexuality, etc.) This contradiction calls into play symbols that mix and even sometimes unite the symbols of life and death into a single image. Those who represent a threat to the spiritual legacy of a community, to the patrilineal line, to the community's control of sexuality or of aggression: these are often represented by symbols associated with death, because they do indeed represent a threat to the survival and continuity of the social order. In one sense, then, it is understandable that religious rituals flirt with death: the flirtation initiates symbolic conquest. Thus it would not be only a religious movement that seems to skirt death: so do the central rites of the nation, whether through sacrifice or through recollections of a critical event like the Passover.

Now, in symbolizing the forces that threaten and oppose a community's survival, a community may be confronting very clear and present dangers; it may also be using symbols to describe imaginary threats: the potential sources of opposition to an otherwise vital and stable social order. The issue for the sociologist very quickly becomes obvious. Do we assume that symbols are somehow symmetrical with a society or in some sort of tension with existing social arrangements? In examining religious beliefs or rituals, is the sociologist looking at a mirror that temporarily distorts a society's actual life in order to enable a society to imagine and overcome threats to its existence? Or is there a fearful symmetry between symbol and social life that allows the sociologist to get a clue to the way things were by examining what is known of its beliefs and practices?[12] In choosing to see symbols as somehow distorting or simply reflecting the institutions and processes of a particular community, a sociologist is likely to adopt what I will be calling the "prophetic" and the "priestly" perspectives on social life. The former orientation tends to distrust myths and symbols, rites and other forms of symbolic action as concealing gaps and contradictions in the life of a society, while the latter (the "priestly") tends to look for consistent patterns and symmetries between a society's culture and its way of life.

Note that this problematic, the relation of language to social life, is also relevant to understanding the Herodian succession, simply because our sources are texts. In this introduction and indeed throughout this book, therefore, I will be raising questions about the relationship of Josephus to his sources, and of the relation of those sources to the world in which they lived. While I have no thought of being able to resolve the existing hermeneutical questions about the utility of Josephus as a source

---

[12] There are other views or paradigms that sociologists might bring to bear on Josephus. See, for instance, how a Marxist viewpoint might inform the study of Josephus: Heinz Kreissig, "A Marxist View of Josephus' Account of the Jewish War," in Feldman 1984: 265–276.

for the period, I will be seeking to demonstrate how a sociologist can work with those questions so that they do not stifle or misdirect sociological inquiry, but provide it with a point of departure.

The relation of language to social life was also problematic for Herod and the people of his period, as indeed it is for any period. None the less the suspicion, the secrecy, the outright distortions and conspiracies of the period warn the sociologist to pay special heed to the problematic relation of any speech, oral or written, to what was actually happening "on the ground," as it were: in the routines but also in the interstices of everyday social life. Indeed, if we are to understand and to interpret what life was like under those circumstances, it will be necessary to perform a leap of the imagination into a world in which it was exceedingly difficult to find someone as good as his or her word. That is, language was not "established," despite the attempt to fix its meaning and prescribe its use in the formulae of the Temple or in contexts like Qumran.

In addressing the problematic relation of language to society, a sociologist will tend to adopt either of what I am calling the "priestly" and "prophetic" viewpoints. Consider, for instance, some fascinating observations made by James Charlesworth (1988) in his recent report of research into the social world of pre-70 CE Palestine. He points out that the entrances to the synagogues of Galilee faced south toward the Jerusalem Temple: a sign that "some allegiance to Jerusalem and its Temple is also demanded by the frequent architectural orientation to the holy city" (1988:115). Others have noted that even in the provinces the bedrooms of many houses were so arranged that the head of someone asleep would point toward the holy city. Does this architectural arrangement signify that there was no opposition between the periphery and the center: that those who worshiped or lived on the periphery were positively oriented toward the Temple, its cult, and the authorities in Jerusalem? From a priestly perspective it would seem logical to assume a certain symmetry between posture and allegiance, but from a prophetic viewpoint it is more probable that orientation of doors and bedrooms reflects what Girard might call "the hostile symmetry of opposites" (especially since in Galilee the northern wall of the synagogue, which Charlesworth [1988:115] calls the "wall of orientation," faced away from Jerusalem). What is needed, I would suggest, is a theory about the various ways that the political and religious center of a nation may be related to the periphery under a variety of conditions; at least with such a theory one could keep open various possible interpretations until other, at first seemingly unrelated observations, had been made and could be called into play.

Clearly the size and orientation of openings are very important, and, as Charlesworth notes, it is helpful to think about them "historically and sociologically, as well as theologically" (1988:115). To think about openings sociologically, of course, is to invite a variety of interpretations, some of them inconsistent with others. On the one hand, for instance, is the work of Mary Douglas, who in "priestly" fashion looks for a certain symmetry between the symbols and facts of social life. From this viewpoint, openings in the Jerusalem Temple or the synagogue would therefore signify places at which the social body, as it were, opens up to receive – or to discharge – its members, as though there were a metabolic process at work in the lives not only of individuals but of the society itself. It therefore matters whether one lives in Jerusalem in a district close to the latrine, as did the Essenes, just as it matters that the Dung Gate was in the southern wall of the old city. Openings on the south side are apparently expressive of what a city wishes to put beyond itself; that could also explain why the northern wall is the "wall of orientation," as Charlesworth so clearly puts it.[13] On this sociological viewpoint there is a symmetry between the archaeological/architectural facts of social life and the ways that individuals interact symbolically with each other in their social (as well as physical) spaces.

On the other hand, however, consider the "prophetic" tendency to look for discrepancies or even contradictions between the way a society is organized symbolically and the way

---

[13] It is interesting to note, in this connection, that in the graves at many ancient Greek sites "The body was placed with its head towards the south" or that the entrance was from the south (Guhl and Koner 1989: 89,99).

individuals and groups actually interact with each other. Those who used to enter the Temple from the south and were oriented northward at that point may have been very suspicious of any influences from the north, just as in Galilee those who used to put the Temple behind them when they entered the synagogue may none the less have been oriented toward the Temple in their sleep.

Ambivalence, inconsistency, and contradiction may also have been the experience of pilgrims who, coming from the periphery, were oriented toward Jerusalem with a mixture of feelings that became more intensely opposed to each other as the holy city came closer. For instance, Victor Turner (1974:182) notes that pilgrims entering the holiest of cities are confronted by the most vivid signs of secularization: the fair, the bazaar, and other evidence of pollution from the world of business and exchange, precisely at the place where one might expect to find signs of sacred order to be predominant. This contradiction between sacred anticipation and secular reality may have been especially painful to pilgrims with mixed emotions about the obligation to make sacrifices in Jerusalem.

To think "sociologically" about the cleansing of the Temple or about the significance of gates and other openings is therefore to open the door to a divergence of viewpoints: some sociologists, like Turner, focus on strains, inconsistencies, and conflicts within social life, while others, more in the Durkheimian mold, seek to demonstrate the symmetries between the way a society is organized, how individuals actually experience their society, and how that experience is symbolized in a wide range of symbols and movements.

I am making a plea against wooden sociological thinking and the use of formal or preconceived typologies. Furthermore, the reality in which people live may or may not be congruous with the truth about their social context; whatever the "reasons" are, in the sense of causes, occasions, or justifications for a particular belief or practice, these "reasons" may not be congruous with the functions, the latent or long-term consequences, of those beliefs and practices. It is far too simple to argue that biblical metaphors of an organic or architectural variety, such as "foundation," "household," or "corner stone," reflect a level of growth and stability in the Christian community, just as apocalyptic metaphors reflect instability, tension, conflict, and change (Kee 1989). Howard Kee assumes that social structures are expressed in beliefs, rather than that the language of religion may romanticize, distort, conceal, or ignore various aspects of social life. Language, as I have already argued, is "slippery"; not even the language of religious discourse can therefore entirely prevent such slippage between the actual and the perceived conditions of social life.

What is needed, I would suggest, is a more flexible sense of the relation of religious beliefs to social life: a sensibility informed by social anthropology and psychoanalysis as well as by the intuitions of faith. Societies which are quite effective (stable, perhaps growing, and well institutionalized) may in fact employ a religious rhetoric that implies the opposite: that is, that would lead one to believe that the continuity of the community itself is continually threatened with terrible dangers from women, sexuality, spirits, individuality, and exchange with outsiders. At times, the Jewish Christian community may indeed have cast Jesus in the role of one who had unusual traffic with women, outsiders, tax collectors, and other such sources of pollution. We could not therefore jump to the conclusion, however, that the boundaries of the community were in fact threatened at that time by outsiders or women, or by other foreign intrusions. As I have just pointed out, communities with stable and secure boundaries often reinforce them by dramatizing the symbolic sources of opposition, regardless of whether any real threat exists to the society's standards and structure. Symbolic enemies are constructed by societies in order for those societies to score symbolic victories over whatever represents the threat of death for the society itself.

My point is that the relationship of language to social identity and to social boundaries cannot be inferred from the meaning of the words themselves. Fragile social boundaries may call forth a language that celebrates secure social boundaries; conversely, boundaries that are secure may be celebrated by rites and in language that imagines them to be insecure and permeable. It is a point that is occasionally overlooked. In raising arguments against the simplistic formulae of Marxists and structuralists, for instance, Kee (1989) would have done well to suggest that even the context, which he takes as a significant clue to the meaning of language, may be quite other than what the words themselves suggest. I think he knows that; it is a question, perhaps, of underemphasis in a short work on sociolinguistics that cannot possibly cover the issues and can name only a few of them. Clearly there is need for a methodological understanding that takes Kee's work and builds on its very real merits in grounding New Testament hermeneutics in social inquiry. In the first chapter I will therefore attempt to explore the differences between "priestly" and "prophetic" sociological paradigms in more detail.

Here I dwell on these alternative sociologies as a means of explaining and interpreting the anguish caused by a succession crisis in the larger society: the breaking-up of a community's spiritual lineage. The point I am making is simply that various outsiders (Galileans, gentiles, women, etc.) do more than "relativize" or call into question one's own righteousness or that of one's lineage. As the opposite of that lineage, the others (gentiles, sexuality, individuality, exchange, etc.) represent the forces of disintegration and of death itself.

Indeed, the opposite of a lineage is likely to be considered to be the moral equivalent of death. When a historian notes that a king or queen is regarded, even in Israel, as the source not only of that nation's peace but of the fertility of its fields, I therefore take it to be highly significant. Not simply an interesting observation, the historian's comment reveals that the nation's people may have attributed to the throne the power to own and control the sources of life itself. Problems in the succession would therefore cause evil: a blight on the land.[14]

---

[14] Schürer–Vermes–Millar (1973: 231–232) observe that Queen Alexandra was credited by the Pharisees with making the fields fertile and productive of extraordinarily large kernels of grain, lentils, and olives. Sin, in this Pharisaic tradition, is the opposite of what a benign and legitimate kingship can provide; sin is conducive to infertility, blighted fields, and the inevitable threat of death. As a sociologist, I see in this historical observation confirmation that at least Pharisaical tradition fits the structuralists' model of how religion symbolizes the threats to a society's continuity and survival in images of decay and death. No wonder, then, that impurity in the body politic, and especially in the kingship as a representative institution of the nation as a whole, should bear such intense symbolic pressure.

To ensure the regeneration of a society from one generation to the next it is crucial not only to manage the succession of the generations; it is also necessary in public rites and speech to close the gap between language and reality. To institutionalize the word, as Max Weber put it, is one of the major functions of religion. Otherwise a society feels itself not only possessed by outside forces that seek to overthrow it , but at the mercy of death itself. Especially in traditional societies, where language rather than the economy or the polity is the dominant institution, a society's faith in itself can be shattered or established according to the establishment of the written and spoken word in concrete social practices. Conversely, those practices, whether of interrogating the elders on the meaning of Torah or of keeping secrets among co-conspirators, can make or break the power of language in a given social context. It is thus impossible to understand social contexts, especially in societies such as Palestine in the first century CE, without appreciating the extent to which a society's ability to reproduce itself from one generation to the next depended on its ownership and control of speech and language.

There is little disagreement that the social context matters, even when that context is as difficult to establish as it is for many biblical texts. It is more difficult still, I would argue, to know what to do with information about the context even when it is available. How do we know when the context matters and when we are dealing with a text addressed to such a wide audience that its provenance is relatively less important than is the context for a liturgy or a song? How do we know what to make of the context even when we know that it matters for the text in question? Without concepts, without a sociological imagination or a scheme for interpreting social life, even the most significant details may seem unrelated to each other. With concepts, however, or with interpretive schemes we may fool ourselves into thinking that we understand these relationships or may think that we see relationships where in fact there are none.

This caveat is especially needed, since Kee (1989) quotes with apparent approval Evans-Pritchard's dictum that "History must choose between being social anthropology and being nothing" (Kee 1989). I am suggesting that even anthropological study of the social context of Scripture is not enough: one must know what to make of that context. However, the sociologists' description, not to mention their interpretation and explanation of the social context of Scripture, will be no better than their grasp of the dynamics of social life, and that grasp is always partial and none too firm even at its best.

Social dynamics can only be properly understood in the additional light shed by disciplines other than sociology and social anthropology. More is at stake, for instance, than what Kee calls the effort of a community to define itself and to bring individuals into this process of self-definition. I am arguing that sociology can truly inform historiography only by combining psychoanalytic insights with social anthropology in a disciplined approach toward limited generalizations. Furthermore, psychoanalytic insights are especially important if one is to grasp what it is actually like to live in a certain time and place.

I have been referring to the work of Howard Kee (1989) because he illustrates a tendency, fairly widespread among biblical scholars who appropriate sociological perspectives, to take rather literally the work of sociologists like Peter Berger, Clifford Geertz, and Mary Douglas, to ignore their internal inconsistencies, and to miss some of the major differences among them. Take Berger, for instance. It is easy to miss the nominalist aspect of Berger's thinking while reading *The Social Construction of Reality*, where it is far less apparent than in *A Rumour of Angels* and *The Precarious Vision*. Indeed, Berger himself seems to vacillate between the two. Again, in reading Mary Douglas it is easy to miss the distinction she draws between the actual structures of social life and how individuals actually experience their social surroundings. Scholars of the New Testament who borrow sociological understandings, I fear, tend to underemphasize the tenuous, variable, and fragmented nature of social experience. For instance, Kee underemphasizes the tentative, "as if" quality of religious belief that makes symbolic construction only "seem" realistic. He is aware of this nominalism in Geertz's work but does not stress it, just as he may be aware of Bellah's work on "the collapse of dualism" but emphasizes the

Bellah who writes as if symbolic worlds are real no matter how unrealistic they may seem to people at any given time or place.

It is very easy to overestimate social structures: in their primacy over the individual in time, in the shaping of reality, and in moral priority. Social life still depends on the social imagination: an imagination which is not easily shaped or contained within social structures, no matter how sacred or well ritualized they may be. Any society still transmutes desire into duty and relies heavily on various forms of sacrifice to ensure compliance. No society can therefore manage a perfect fit between individuals and the roles they occupy, nor can any society so thoroughly institutionalize language as to make all promises and commitments seem beyond doubt or cavil of any kind. At the heart of many societies is a fantasy world of imaginary rights and duties, entitlements and honors, and it is in this world that many individuals still live, regardless of how rationally they fulfill their stated duties. That is why sociology must combine psychoanalytic with social anthropological insights if we are to understand not only the existential significance of social life but the discontents that accompany any civilizing processes.

As a sociologist in a theological seminary, I believe that theologians can and should inform sociological analysis with a perspective that challenges simplistic views of human nature and social life; there are many such in sociology in need of challenge, including the evolutionary systems theory associated with such figures as Parsons and Niklas Luhmann. And I also believe that a theology that relies on a simplistic view of "the world," as a polar term to "the church," will also be trivialized, unless and until the world is plumbed and searched with the same love and intensity that theologians bring to the Scriptures.

CHAPTER I

Two methodological viewpoints: the priestly and the prophetic

In approaching antiquity, students of Christian origins will be approaching a very strange world indeed. Fortunately, however, other communities, equally strange but closer to our own time, have been studied in depth by social anthropologists. Their descriptions can at least open up a set of questions for us to pursue as we study the far less accessible world of first-century Palestine. In this chapter, for instance, I will rely heavily on two recent works by social anthropologists; both of them focus on ways that traditional communities seek to secure for themselves the sources of life from one generation to the next.

SOCIETAL SELF-REPRODUCTION

To guarantee that a community will continue despite the death of its members over time is not easy. Each community must be sure, for instance, of its own spiritual continuity with the past. In this chapter we will note how a community seeks to ensure that the spirit of the ancestors lives on in the new-born, fertilizes its fields, endows its leaders with authority and holds off the threat of evil and death from the community itself. It is as if those who have died possess the secret of the community's life and remain the sources of its vitality. Access to the dead means ownership and control over the sources of life.[1] That is a strange world

[1] On the "Tabula Hebana" a bill was carved to "ensure that offerings are made to the departed spirit of Germanicus [Caesar], a decree quite typical of respects shown to members of the Augustan imperial family" (Braund 1985: 55; cf. 37–38). It was customary in such bills and decrees to lavish honorific titles on the member of the imperial family, like "father of the country," "son of a god," *pontifex maximus*, "*princeps* of youth," etc. The line of descent clearly links the regeneration of the community from one generation to the next with the imperial descent from divine ancestors.

indeed to moderns, who live in a world that tends to separate the living from the dead and to locate the sources of a community's vitality as much in its skills and achievements as in its cultural inheritance. Modern societies also worry about their access to the sources of life, but these are found in the environment, in access to capital and to scientific techniques and technology, as well as in the inherited capital, so to speak, of ideas and values from the past. In this chapter, then, I wish to commend to students of the Bible a recent study by a group of social anthropologists who have examined a wide range of traditional communities – some tightly knit, others quite loosely constructed – in search of some basic understanding of how such communities perpetuate themselves. I am referring to Bloch and Parry's 1982 work, *Death and the Regeneration of Life*.

Before going on, I should add a word about why I have chosen this text rather than any of the others that might have served the same purpose, that is, to supply illustrations of communities that might serve to raise the right questions about Palestinian society in the first century. The descriptions in Bloch and Parry's book are informed by the notion that ideology is the right term to substitute for culture. It is a prophetic notion: that is, it carries with it a number of critical assumptions about the relation of culture to community life. One of those assumptions is that culture (i.e. ideology) serves to edit reality: something is always left out. Another assumption is that ideology serves to conceal or cover contradictions in the life of a community: contradictions, however, that the community must face if it is to survive and even prosper. That is because ideology is a compromise with reality itself: an assertion of continuity in the face of change, of life in the face of death. Like any such compromise with reality, then, ideology is symptomatic of conflicts that have not been faced directly and resolved. These conflicts and contradictions, I would add, are inescapable and universal: for example, the contradictions between a society's structure and its processes, between the given aspects of social life and the spontaneous, between the requirements of the community for continuity and its requirements for adapting to changes within and outside its boundaries. Being inescapable and universal, these conflicts may also be located in first-century Palestine, where the succession of a society from one generation to the next was no less problematic than it is in any of the societies studied by Bloch, Parry, and their associates.

In this chapter I wish also to commend another recent compilation of studies by social anthropologists: Parkin's *The Anthropology of Evil* (1985). Like the first book I have mentioned, it has the virtue of combining two kinds of interpretation. On the one hand, it is important to know *how things hang together*; for instance, how does the respect accorded to ancestors serve to perpetuate the community? Is the line of descent preserved intact, at the expense primarily of women who marry into the family? Or are the ancestors who preserve the continuity of the community likely to be benign toward those who are brought in by marriage? Needless to say, in a study of Christian origins, it is important to know how the preservation of a house affects – and is affected by – the preservation of a lineage. It is also important, however, to interpret social life in a way that goes to the heart of human experience. *What is it like* to live in a world where marriage is a threat to the continuity of the community, and where outsiders bring the threat of pollution and death? To know what people do and say, how they feel about and how they interpret their own practices is the first task not only of the social anthropologist but of all who claim to minister to others.

Parkin and his colleagues are committed to understanding the sense that people make of their own experience: what they consider to be the sources of their own well-being and the sources of premature death and blighted lives. I find their work particularly useful for raising questions about communities in first-century Palestine, where the well-being of communities was of such critical importance to the salvation of individuals, and where the well-being of individuals guaranteed the continuity and succession of the community from one generation to the next. The disease of Herod, for instance, could bring down not only his house but the lineage and, with the lineage, the continuity of the kingship itself. On the other hand, the succession might be found in others who could demonstrate the extraordinary charisma of messianic kings.

Any society has to maintain itself against all sorts of forces that would threaten and disrupt its continuity from one generation to the next. The contributors to *Death and the Regeneration of Life* note that each community must come to terms with the dead. The ancestors are an essential source of life and fertility; the continuing life of the community depends on their blessing. Otherwise crops would fail and women would be sterile. The continuity from one generation to the next is indeed at the mercy of ancestors, whose favor can be withdrawn if they are not properly treated. Imagine, then, how disruptive it must have been for Jesus to say, "let the dead bury the dead" (Luke 9:60).

On the other hand, the dead themselves can be disruptive: a frightening, unwanted element in everyday life. Even in homes that preserve ancestral bones under the floor, the living can only enjoy that part of a house that is not in fact a sepulcher. Latvians in Canada, furthermore, often make arrangements to have their own ashes sent back to the old country for burial; otherwise they seek to have a container of soil from the old country placed at their grave in Canada. Where the life of the person depends on the community, and the community in turn is rooted in a locale, the dead must be treated very properly if life is to go on each day and from one generation to the next. Indeed, in Josephus' account of Herod's fatal errors, none seems more important than Herod's violation of the tomb of David; it prefigures Herod's inability to appease the souls of close members of his family, whom he murders in his desperation over ensuring the succession.

It is inevitable that the fragile unity between the generations will be disturbed. To begin with, no lineage can perpetuate itself without going outside itself through marriage; otherwise the lineage flirts with incest and with marriage within the "prohibited degrees of consanguinity." The ideal remains: a line must go on without interruption. The fact also remains that outsiders must come in. The "in-laws" are a category that stays, even in a mobile and secular society such as our own, the object of fear and joking. It is women, furthermore, who must enter into a patriarchal lineage from outside. The contributors to this collection often find the women associated with disruption.

They are the ones with consuming passions, whether these passions are associated with sexuality or even with the fear of cannibalism (Bloch and Parry 1982: 126). Certainly in Herod's household the women appear to be the sources of disruption. In Josephus' view it is the women whose gossip, ambition, and sexuality disturb the line of succession from father to son. They are an uncontrollable source of disruption in the lineage. Josephus is therefore revealing the dominant ideology in the Judaism of the time, whether or not his accounts of the facts about particular women are to be believed. Note, in this connection, the prominence of women within the Jesus movement. Were they present as a symbolic threat to patri-lineage?

Any ideology that seeks to preserve the life-giving connection between the generations and between the living and the dead must therefore come to terms with certain contradictions. As I have already noted (and as Bloch and Parry point out in their introduction), the dead are often disruptive: note the care taken at the time of Halloween and All Saints to manage their return without more than the necessary heartache and turbulence.[2] The murder of Mariamme, the mother of the two sons destined at first to succeed Herod, is at the heart of the anguish and conflict in that royal household; her spirit is never fully laid to rest, as it were. As for the other disruptions caused by the women, it is Salome's flirtation with a visiting Arab that later makes the Herodian household vulnerable to subversion at Caesar's court, just as it is Salome's greed and destructiveness that causes the death of John the Baptist. The gospels themselves are written in a world where the spirits of the dead, like those of the prophets, return to unsettle the society, especially when its

---

[2] Josephus noted that Rome was in considerable turmoil after the assassination of Gaius Caesar Augustus; soldiers, aspirants to the throne, and fellow conspirators posed a considerable threat to the senate, and the future of the senate itself was at stake. Claudius, the successor to Gaius, pardoned one of the assassins, Sabinus, and had another, Chaerea, executed after he was condemned by his companions, who none the less "considered his action to be splendid." After the execution of Chaerea "the people of Rome . . . honoured Chaerea with portions placed on his pyre, calling upon him to be mild and not angry at the ingratitude shown towards him [for his popular assassination of Gaius]" (*Antiquities* xix.248–273; quoted in Braund 1985: 81–83).

lines of succession are disrupted. The gospels also reflect the ambiguous and dangerous position of women in a society that regenerates itself through succession from father to son.

What is sought ideally is a world that owns and controls its own sources of life: the spirit of the ancestors who guarantee fertility and new generations yet unborn; the prosperity of the community without exchange with outsiders; biological life without corruption and impurity. Clearly every society, however, must face the unpleasant legacies of the ancestors, the facts of social and economic exchange without outsiders, and inevitable decay and corruption. The ideal is therefore enacted in rituals that promise continuity, regeneration, and a victory over death and corruption: witness the Passover and Pentecost, for instance, as celebrations in the first century that brought thousands of pilgrims to Jerusalem for precisely such symbolic enactments. In these rites the faithful are reminded that their ancestors murdered an Egyptian but were saved from the plague that passed over them; they celebrate the renewal of the fields and rejoice in new plantings. On the other hand, some attend the feasts only to engage in economic exchange with the pilgrims; the fact that the community depends on exchange with outsiders inevitably has an impact on the community's self-understanding. It is possible, for instance, that the pilgrimages were a ritualized means of allowing for exchange with outsiders who were, for the duration of the pilgrimage, given the status of insiders and who thus no longer posed a symbolic threat to the purity of the community and nation.

It is only men, of course, who engage in these rites: the women, like those men who are too old or too young, are excluded from the celebration. There is a spirit, in other words, that proceeds from father to son and that guarantees the line of descent against interruption and death itself, despite the threat of women, mere commercial exchange, and death itself. So the community is renewed at these festivals. When they are disrupted, as they were at the time of Herod's death, it is the succession of the entire community and not of the royal dynasty alone that is at stake: especially so if, as in Jesus' entry into

Jerusalem at the Passover-time, there are rival claimants to royal charisma.[3]

To have access to the sources of life is the religious mission of virtually every belief-system; to manage and to control these sources of life is an intrinsically political mission. The combination of the religious and the political characterizes traditional societies in a way that is difficult for a modern to comprehend, even in the light of the messianic politics of left- and right-wing Christian groups in the West. In Herod's time, for instance, Caesar was a "friend" and "redeemer": the savior of the world. For Herod himself, in fact, Augustus had been his "redeemer" in saving him from his enemies; Augustus had also made Herod king of the Jews.[4] As Cornfeld (1982:90) points out,

> Rome under Augustus was marked by a sense of achievement, which inspired all the emperor's subjects to feel that he was "the man the world needed." For most outside Italy, membership within the empire induced a sense of receiving direction from an earthly "providence."

Of course Herod would seek to build monuments to Augustus in many Hellenistic cities; his record as a builder of monuments is simply prodigious. Cornfeld (1982) records the efforts of Herod to insure the place of Israel within the Roman empire and to insure his own position within the Roman-Hellenistic elite. In tribute to Caesar he built Caesarea, an extraordinary port on the Mediterranean with advanced engineering and facilities for trade; there he also placed a superb statue of Caesar that resembled Zeus himself (Cornfeld 1982:83). There were

---

[3] Other authors have made a direct connection between the insurrections that occurred at the time of Herod's death and the later insurrections occurring continually from those at the death of Archelaus (6 CE) to the civil war in 66–73/4 CE. See Nikiprowetsky, "Josephus and the Revolutionary Parties," in Feldman and Hata 1989: 225.

[4] "Most Jews did not regard Herod as a 'Jewish king' of established Jewish descent, namely that of the 'House of David,' as the Pharisees would have it, but as '*a king of the Jews*,' appointed by Rome, and a loyal protector of the gentiles in his realm" (Cornfeld 1982: 112 [n. 571(a)]).

other monuments in cities outside as well as within Israel: fountains, pools, columns, porticoes, theaters, amphitheaters, markets (Cornfeld 1982: 87ff.). The project of Herod, I am arguing, was the same as that of any traditional society, that is, to create a public sphere which promises ownership and control of the sources of life. Note especially, therefore, his building of the Temple in Jerusalem.

Part of that project, of course, is to ensure continuity with the ancestors, whose presence is a necessary, if not sufficient guarantee, of the continuity of life itself over the generations. Josephus puts it succinctly; in Cornfeld's translation:

Having immortalized the memory of his family and friends, he did not neglect to ensure his own memory for posterity. (1982: 87; *Jewish War* 1.21.10)

That is, the landscape of Israel was defined by these monuments: a city named after Herod's father (Antipatris), a fortification dedicated to his mother, another city named after his brother, and a tower to the same brother in Jerusalem itself (*Jewish War* 1.21.9; Cornfeld 1982:86). The land itself, then, becomes defined by monuments and entire cities that seek to guarantee the flow of life from the past within the present. Thus the boundaries between the living and the dead become diffuse and overlap each other. The dead are honorary citizens, as it were, of the kingdom: notables to whom honor is due and from whom benefits are expected. Not to honor them could be revolutionary. Thus for the Jesus movement to withhold honors due the dead, by suggesting "Let the dead bury their dead" (Luke 9:60), was a threat to the society's own means of reproducing itself over time and would have been given the appropriate punishment.

To a modern it may seem extreme to argue that these monuments define a society's lineage and therefore shape its notions of legitimate authority. Bloch and Parry argue, however, that in traditional societies funerary monuments are a means of disposing of the unwanted or threatening aspects of an individual while laying claim to what is essential to the continuity and vitality of a society. Tombs themselves "are used to construct an idealized material map of the permanent social order" (Bloch and Parry 1982: 35). None the less, a degree of methodological skepticism is in order: let me explain.

PRIESTLY AND PROPHETIC METHODOLOGY

From a methodological viewpoint that I would call "prophetic" it stands to reason that any society will have flaws, gaps, and contradictions. The methodological point is to look for exceptions, deviant cases, ways in which the "idealized" order of a society breaks down in practice or covers more specific, particular interests that cloak themselves in the common good. To a methodologist of the prophetic persuasion, it comes as no surprise to find that, as Bloch and Parry point out,

the growth in the size and significance of royal tombs seems to be accompanied by a diminution, or even a total eradication, of the tombs of the subjects as permanent objects. (1982:35)

Think of the implications of this comment, which they offer only "in passing." Far from a passing interest of the methodologist, it is precisely this erosion of the importance of other centers of loyalty and authority that is of significance. In the Palestinian case, the expansion of the political center under Herod would have threatened the authority of families whose shrines and tombs may have been on the same land for hundreds of years.[5]

There is a contradiction, then, between the monuments of the center and those on the periphery. On the periphery, furthermore, there may have been wells and grottoes: a variety of earth shrines and fertility cults that offered access to the sources of life that were neither owned nor controlled by the center. Indeed, Turner (1979) in his studies of pilgrimage has noted the ancient competition of the shrines of the earth with those of the *polis*, just as Burkert (1979) has commented on the rivalry between the family ties to a peripheral or rural locale and the demands of the

[5] Note that Herod Antipas had built Tiberias on the site of an ancient cemetery. There could hardly have been a more drastic severing of the ties between the past and the present or a more flagrant provocation to insurrection in that part of the kingdom. No wonder that relatively few Jews and a large number of "foreigners, adventurers, and beggars" lived in this Hellenistic city: Schürer–Vermes–Millar 1973: 342–343.

political center for a monopoly on the lines of authoritative succession. The center's lineage prevails over the other lineages of the country, unless countermovements manage to assert their own lineages and the authority of ancestral houses of their own.

From what I have called a "priestly" methodological perspective, however, even these contradictions can be subsumed in patterns of adherence and devotion. A central calendar can prescribe days of obligation and the occasions for sacrifice that unite the periphery to the center. Jewish males, who stood directly in the lines of succession, were obliged to make pilgrimages three times annually to the central shrine in Jerusalem, the Temple. They brought the signs of fertility with them: the first fruits of the field and the herd, which were offered at the Temple itself. The center claimed the right to perform the sacrifices of praise and thanksgiving for the fertility of the land in feasts such as Pentecost, which fell only fifty days after the national rite of praise and thanksgiving for the salvation of the nation from Egyptian domination and the plague, i.e. from death itself.

On the other hand, there remained deviant religious movements on the periphery which withheld sacrifice, refused to honor the center at stated times of the year, and which claimed to have an authoritative spiritual lineage of their own priesthood; the prime example, of course, is the Essene movement. Even these antithetical sources of religious and national legitimacy, however, would be treated – in the logic of a priestly methodology – as sources of a dynamic in which the center both corresponds to and transcends the periphery; whereas the socio-logic of a prophetic methodology would see the periphery as a source of contradiction not easily transcended or subsumed by the symbols and liturgies of the nation's center.

OBLIGATION: THE SUCCESSION-CRISIS AND THE MANAGEMENT OF DEATH

The prophetic method searches for contradictions or at least for discrepancies and gaps in a society. It may focus, for instance, on gaps between professed religious ideals and actual practices.

Religious virtuosos, for instance, seek to live as though they did not need to concern themselves with mundane activities and the details of everyday life; as Weber often reminded us, the obligations of devotees to religious virtuosos like mystics and wonder-workers were intended to keep up the myth that the true believer need not worry about what he or she will eat or drink. The prophetic orientation therefore likes to find instances of rational or pragmatic calculation in the life and work of the Ghandis of this world. This comment by Jonathan Parry is typical of the prophetic approach; he notes

the familiar South Asian contradiction that, while the ascetic is enjoined to remain completely independent of the material and social order, he must necessarily depend on the gifts of the householder to support himself, and can therefore never entirely escape from the lay world. (Bloch and Parry 1982: 97)

There is nothing here to indicate why this contradiction is typically South Asian rather than typical of all religious virtuosos. Mystics and wonder-workers still have to eat and seek shelter, even while attempting to regenerate themselves and to transcend death by minimizing their sexual needs, their individuality, and their exchanges with the world. None the less, Parry's focus on contradictions is methodologically "prophetic."

Of course, few collections are likely to be pure in their method. One of the contributors to Bloch and Parry's collection, Mr. Strathern, is inclined to find consistent patterns among the inhabitants of New Guinea. He notes that they are likely to pay their obligations and to engage in exchange; in fact, they are suspicious of women and Europeans because both groups seem to take rather than to give. This tendency toward healthy-minded exchange is expressed in several practices: for example, "when a child is weaned and its hair is first cut, the father is expected to make a payment to his wife's kin" (Strathern 1982: 120). It would appear to some New Guinea Highlanders, for example, the Melpa, that there are creatures who consume greedily rather than engage in fair exchanges; these are likely to be witches, ghosts, and cannibals. Now, how does one explain variations among these tribes in their willingness to engage in exchanges with outsiders? One methodology, the prophetic, will look for an explanation in the covert contradictions of the community; the other methodology, the priestly, will try to find symmetries between the way a society is constructed and how it construes foreign exchange.

Some New Guineans, for instance, are far less inclined than the Melpa (in the example above) to exchange with outsiders: consider the wary Etero. This tribe is more endogamous, and, Strathern argues, therefore more agreeable to the practice of cannibalism. The difference between the two is due to the relatively tightly knit, small, and endogamous social life of the Etero tribe, whose vital essences must be retained among themselves, whereas the Melpa are somewhat more complex in their relationships with outsiders and therefore engage in exchange as if their life depended on it. The point is that Strathern looks for a consistent pattern between the tribe's beliefs and its social organization rather than for gaps and contradictions. That is what I would call the "priestly" method.

Like editors of any collection, Bloch and Parry are not eager to allow too many methodological variations among their contributors. Why should Parry, in his piece on ascetics, look for contradictions, while Strathern is allowed to find consistent patterns between societies and their cultures? In their introduction, therefore, the editors argue that what Strathern has *really* found is a similarity between two quite different groups:

the Etero practice [cannibalism] corresponds to the Melpa phantasy of an enviable order without exchange – an order which they create in their rituals but which their society, based on the foundation of exchange, makes impossible. (Bloch and Parry 1982: 31)

The editors are focusing on an impossible ideal: the ideal, that is, of a society enabled to regenerate itself by its own patterns of consumption, production, and reproduction, without reliance on exchange, on women from other communities, and without disturbance from individuals, sexuality, and chance itself. The Melpa actually engage in exchange, and yearn for a self-sufficient social order, but project that wish on to witches and cannibals, who do manage to be both self-sufficient and all-consuming. It is easier for the Melpa to express the wish as a fear than to confront it directly, especially when the world is not organized to satisfy such wishes for an inexhaustible environment subject to unlimited consumption. The prophetic methodology of the editors comes to the fore in their comparison of the Melpa's ideals or "surreptitious yearning" with their reality or with another community's (the Etero's) actual practice.

A prophetic methodology focuses on the basic contradiction between the reality of the need for exchange with outsiders and the ideal of complete autonomy. The communal goal is to have things go smoothly in an uncertain world, and any disturbance is thus a source of pollution. The priestly orientations of a particular society are therefore most easily debunked by a prophetic sociological method. I should note that the reverse is also true, i.e. that a society's apparent gaps and contradictions can be harmonized by sociologists who see patterns or at least functions working for the benefit of the society as a whole, regardless of partial or temporary dislocations and conflicts.

Such methodological differences separate those who would see in the Jesus movement the fulfillment of the Torah or, conversely, its supersession. The difference is methodological, and it has perpetuated years of argumentation among New Testament scholars. It would require a separate volume to review that literature and to suggest a resolution of the discussion. Here I can only hope to lay out a few methodological ground-rules for those employing a socio-logic in the effort to reconstruct the texts in the light of their times.

THE SOURCES OF OBLIGATION

From the priestly viewpoint, the sources of obligation are intrinsic to social life. It is individuals who are indeed the creatures of their societies: they owe their origin, their birth, their growth, their maturity, their continuity and livelihood, their vitality and identity, to their social systems; after death they depend on the proper rites to usher them through a new birth, into the world of the departed. Those who do not receive the proper attention after their deaths may come back to haunt

their communities; Olivia Harris' (1982: 45ff.) discussion of the
Laymi makes it very clear that individuals receive considerable
attention after death, lest they return to claim their own,
whatever "their own" may be: a child, possessions, food, the
land itself. There is a certain reciprocity between the living and
the dead that redresses the imbalance of obligation between the
individual and the society in this life. For the living, however, to
pay one's dues to the dead is to own up to one's obligations to
one's society for life itself:

> each ethnic group apparently venerated its own ancestors, or at least
> those of the lords, often embalmed or in the form of an "idol," and held
> sacred the tombs or the caves where the relics and images were
> preserved. These ranked high in the indigenous pantheon, and
> bestowed strength, good fortune, and prosperity on those who
> worshipped them . . . Small wonder that so much missionary energy
> was directed towards this fundamental source of social existence.
> (Harris 1982: 46)

Note that the source of contradiction (the missionary) here is
external to the society. From the priestly methodological
viewpoint, contradictions enter in from the outside and create a
disturbance in the smooth functioning of the system which, left
to its own ritual devices, can perpetuate itself through performing the proper obsequies to the living and, most importantly, to
the dead. To "let the dead bury the dead" or to believe in an
empty tomb would be to cut one's ties with the community of
origin, once and for all.

There are theoretical reasons for preferring the priestly
method. If one is indebted to Durkheimian sociology, for
instance, the method assumes what Durkheim set out to prove:
that is, that societies are the source of moral obligation and the
proper object, therefore, of a sense of duty. Societies are the
source of obligation because the individual (ontologically
speaking) is quite simply a social product; societies are the object
of a sense of duty because, in the next-to-last analysis, social life,
society itself, is a psychic phenomenon and exists (phenom-
enologically speaking, of course) within the mind of the
individual.

What are we to make, then, of Olivia Harris' report, in the

piece just cited, that the Laymi described their ancestors as "devils" without making it clear to her that the devils were really their ancestors in disguise? Their identity was implicitly understood within their culture until festal music revealed them at the end of months of hard labor and heavy duty. The answer, from the priestly viewpoint, is that the intrusion of Christianity rendered the departed somewhat alien to the human group: clearly part of the prohibited world to which the church raised conscientious objection. The dead could visit the community only if they were disguised as the devils which, in the eyes of the missionaries, indeed they were. The sources of contradiction between the past and the present, between the living and the dead, and between generations were therefore made external to the group itself. Thus an alien religion further alienated the living from the dead. From a prophetic viewpoint, however, there is always a contradiction and a potential conflict between the living and the dead, just as there is conflict between the generations. It is endemic and internal to the society, and the conflict can only be externalized by going through the motions of make-believe and ritualized dramatization. On this view the impact of the missionaries may have been to make it necessary to disguise the identity of the Laymi's ancestors, but the internal struggle between the living and the dead would have been present regardless of the intrusion of other foreigners into the Laymi's world.

The difference between the two methodological starting points, the priestly and the prophetic, becomes clearer when we examine a discussion that self-consciously contrasts its own viewpoint, the prophetic, with a more priestly or Durkheimian approach. Maurice Bloch, in the following passage, is discussing what he calls the "generally received anthropological wisdom that death is a challenge to the social order" (1982: 218). On the contrary, he goes on to argue, it is death on which the social order depends in order to create itself in the social imagination of those taking part, for instance, in funeral rites:

The ideal image is constructed by constructing a phantasmagoric ritually-constructed antithesis – the world of women, pollution, sorrow and individuality. Then once created dramatically this world is vanquished by the right order of midday, the triumph of the regrouping in the tomb . . . Death as disruption, rather than being a problem for the social order, as anthropologists have tended to think of it, is in fact an opportunity for dramatically creating it. (1982: 218–219)

There are several elements of the prophetic viewpoint in this argument. The first is that the social order is seen as a dramatic production: a cultural fiction in which many believe as a result of taking part in the process of producing it through ritual. Secondly it is the individuals who – as producers – are real, and the society represents the surplus value, as it were, of their cultural labors: a value that is then expropriated for the legitimation of the priests and kings who present themselves as the guardians of social order. In the third place, the prophetic viewpoint engages in a hermeneutics of debunking "this *apparent* permanence . . . created by the denial of the main discontinuous processes in the social group, i.e. death" (1982: 219). The reality of disruption by death is in fact denied by the cultural fiction of a permanence achieved through symbolic victories over death itself. (On this view, the death and resurrection of Jesus could be seen as a drama performed for the revitalization of Israel.)

Finally, this order is costly: someone has to pay for it. Those who pay the highest price are those who are used as foils for the ritualized dramatization of the triumph of the social order. These foils or stage props are the dead, but they also include women and the young: anyone, in fact, who can represent the antithesis of social order and so be brought in as stage-props for the dramatic production and reproduction of order in the face of opposition. Speaking of "the symbolic construction of a deme" (the people and the land of the Merina) united and victorious over time, decay, and death, Maurice Bloch goes on to say:

Birth and death in their deme aspect are the same. This symbolic collapse of apparent opposites then becomes one of the main elements in the permanent construction of the eternal deme. Indeed, the very notion of the permanent association of undivided people with undivided land, unaffected by time requires this collapse. One can say, therefore, that in Merina ideology the concepts of birth and death are systematically collapsed in these rituals and made one by opposing them to an antithesis acted out by women, biological birth and biological death. In the ideological construction nothing is born, nothing dies and therefore nothing is transformed or legitimately transformable. (1982: 220)

That is the key point, that is, that there is no legitimate basis for opposition to a society that subsumes all its opposites into one unity. Ideology makes the remaining sources of contradiction external to the society's model of itself; the price of legitimacy is therefore paid by the representatives of a natural order that lies outside the social. These representatives are women, biological processes, sexuality, and death itself. An alienated society estranges itself from its internal sources of conflict and locates them in enemies such as demons or an imperial power: for example, Beelzebub and Rome (see Mark 4: 22ff.; 5: 1–20). In these demonic or political forms, as, for instance, Legion or Beelzebub, the internal contradictions of Palestinian society could be externalized and defeated by a movement claiming to regenerate the community or nation as a whole.

From a priestly viewpoint this process is one of evolution. As societies emerge and develop, they do in fact become differentiated from the natural order. The priestly viewpoint does not ignore conflict within a society or the role of those in power in defining and resolving such conflict for their own continued benefit. None the less, the emphasis of this methodological starting point is on searching for a consistent pattern. Such consistency is interesting for two reasons. On the one hand it may suggest a normative order which runs throughout a society and transcends all conflicts and differences. After all, the women who are portrayed as the source of opposition, decay, and individuality in the societies examined by Bloch and his associates also bear the major responsibilities for mourning and the care of corpses. They co-operate, as it were, in their own suppression because there is in fact a normative order that is exhibited in quite consistent patterns of behavior across a wide range of societies.[6]

---

[6] Note that under the Hasmoneans women for the first time ruled as queens and shared the authority of kingship, although they were excluded from the high priesthood and therefore unable to consolidate power in their own hands. Their relationship to political power was therefore ambiguous, since they were both insiders and outsiders; that is perhaps why judgments on Hasmonean queens like Salome Alexandra are somewhat confusing and ambiguous. See Sievers 1989: 132–146.

Bloch (1982: 224ff.) notes "that in those societies focussed on traditional authority there will . . . always be a double aspect to funerals." That double aspect is simply the decay and disintegration of what belongs to nature versus the continuity of the social order. What belongs to nature may be the flesh, while the social order is represented by the bone; the same dichotomy separates the individual and women (both "flesh") from the ancestral soul and men (both "bone").

In other words, the primitive differentiation of society from nature accounts for this "double aspect" in the mythology and rites surrounding death. The principal order is of ancestors, of a royal lineage, or of a people indissolubly associated with the land, yet separate from the land to the extent that the people has a social order whose rhythms and continuity are not wholly dependent on nature. The anomalies are pushed, like women and children or corpses, to the side, but they are not really sources of opposition or of fundamental contradiction. (On this view the inclusion of women in the Jesus movement would be less revolutionary than anomalous.)

It follows that, in a society whose rhythms, vagaries, and fate are less differentiated from nature, the social order itself will seem more contingent, less continuous, and less suitable, therefore, for ritual dramatization. The same may be said, however, of the most complex and "advanced" societies: their orders, too, are difficult to dramatize in ritual and thus seem difficult to control or comprehend. At the extremes, then, the most "differentiated" societies resemble the least coherent and continuous forms of "primitive" social organization. Among hunters and gatherers, for instance, as among the mobile and transient dwellers of certain metropolitan areas in the West, individuals have relatively little to hope for or to fear from one another; relationships are short-term, obligations limited and temporary, and duties to the living and the dead are specific and easily disposed of: what I have called elsewhere a secular society. James Woodburn has noted that among hunters and gatherers there are "few formal obligations or commitments to the living and few, too, to the dead and accordingly few opportunities to wrong the living or the dead" (1982: 207).

Note the emphasis here on the way the system works as a system, so that a kind of rationality informs economic and ritualized actions and yields consistency of pattern. That is what I mean by a priestly methodological orientation. It finds consistency of pattern between symbols and social life whether one is examining a society that is dependent on the seasons or one that is highly separate from the natural order. Both will find their symbols in the variable and shifting aspects of nature itself; whereas for the prophetic sociologist nature serves as a storehouse of symbols to disguise the constraints and contradictions of social life and to make them seem "natural."

What, then, of societies that are neither primitive nor advanced? Take, for example, societies with well-established kingships and orderly successions from one generation to the next. Funerals are a strategic moment for the investigation of any society, and particularly for societies in which ritual does indeed dramatize the enduring aspects of social order. At the funeral of the king, for instance, one can examine the world of obligations and ask whether they are long-term or short-term. From a priestly viewpoint, one might expect to find a society, through its rites of succession, exhibiting its continuities over time and its roots in the natural order; obligations will therefore be seen as given, fixed in the order of things, and renewed through the accession of a new ruler to the throne. The sources of conflict will be transcended in ritual, and the new order will guarantee new sources of tribute for the king and of life, vitality, fertility, and security for the people. From a prophetic viewpoint one would expect to find what some call the "manufacture of consensus" during such rites of succession: the attempt to create the fiction of legitimate authority, the illusion of continuity, and a new web of obligation binding the ruled to the rulers. Contradictions will be glossed over, and the sources of conflict made to seem external to the social order itself, for example, in the intrusions of those who represent the forces of disintegration, decay, and death. As I shall note, the rites of the succession of Archelaus to the throne left empty at the death of Herod are open to just such contrary interpretations.

APPLYING THESE TWO METHODOLOGIES TO THE HERODIAN SUCCESSION

Rather than simply set these two viewpoints (the priestly and the prophetic) off against each other, however, I would like to suggest a strategy for weighing them in the balance of certain kinds of evidence. The prophetic viewpoint searches for evidence of distortions in the process of communication. To conceal gaps and contradictions, the relevant speakers will necessarily have to elaborate in complex ways at high levels of abstraction, use symbols to distract and to delude their hearers, sanctify paradox and irony, or become circumspect if not altogether silent. Words will not have their intended effect, and speakers will not be taken at their word. The priestly viewpoint, however, expects the process of communication to reflect and in turn recreate the social order. It therefore expects vows and promises, acclamations and oaths, to reinforce the bonds between rulers and the ruled; the succession will go smoothly because the sequences of speaking, hearing and responding will have been sustained and completed. As the rituals of succession proceed smoothly to their conclusion, the social order will have reproduced itself once again not only *despite* the intrusion of death but, as we have noted, precisely *because* death provides the occasion for such a recreation of the social order. Recreation occurs through rites of word and deed: symbolic acts of tribute and of duty that create a new world of obligation and guarantee the succession from one ruler and generation to the next.

The death of Herod provides us, then, with a strategic moment in which to assess the relation of language to social reality in first-century Palestine: "strategic" because so much that is latent at other times becomes manifest when a society must ensure its own continuity through rites of succession. Josephus' account (*Antiquities* XVII.8 and 9) is particularly useful because it focuses on the exchange of tribute, promises, vows, and acclamations: the linguistic acts that make or break a succession and illumine a society's gaps and contradictions as well as the outlines of its order. *Antiquities* XVII.8 focuses on the acclamations and promises. The multitude seem to be competing with themselves to raise the loudest shouts of praise to Herod's son, Archelaus. In turn, Archelaus thanks them for not demanding recompense for the injuries they had sustained from his father. As a kinder and gentler speech from Herod's son raises hopes for a less repressive regime, Josephus notes, the more the people ask for the release of political prisoners and the reduction of various taxes that had been imposed by Herod.

Josephus' suspicions about the relation of speech to reality, however, are quite apparent in his own account of these occasions; at one point he notes:

> To these demands Archelaus made no opposition, for he was eager to do anything to please the multitude in the belief that the goodwill of the people would greatly help to preserve his power. Thereupon he sacrificed to God and betook himself to feasting with friends. (*Antiquities* xvii.8.4; *Josephus* 1969: 467)

It is not clear at this point whether Josephus himself is employing the prophetic method to which I referred earlier; his observation is quite simple in itself, however: Archelaus avoided expressing the contradictions in the social order that divided the people from his regime and could upset his succession to the throne.

Josephus' own account is no doubt informed by a mixture of biases, not all of them mutually compatible, and in this book I will have occasion to comment on the methodological problems occasioned by such an account. Here it is enough for the moment to underscore the importance of his observations on whether public discourse reflects or distorts the social reality that it seeks to recreate. A prophetic viewpoint, of course, would find Josephus' account of Archelaus' pretensions and feigned good-will to be sufficient evidence of an official's attempt to gloss over social contradictions with honeyed speech.

Josephus' account can be read another way, however. After all, Archelaus must first go to Rome to have his accession to the throne ratified by Caesar; any promises in the mean time must be tentative, whether or not they are in good faith. Archelaus himself sent a general to the people to remind them that clamor for concessions would be seen as subversive prior to Caesar's ratification of Archelaus' claim to the kingship: an attempt at silencing the multitude which prompted the multitude in their turn to silence the general (*Antiquities* xvii.9.1, 2). Here it seems to be the multitude who are disturbing what could have been the orderly process of succession, in which the will of Caesar would have ramified through the provinces and down the legitimate lines of authority to restore peace, public order, and justice. So would go an explanation informed by a priestly methodological viewpoint.

The occasion for this last disturbance, however, is revealing. Josephus notes that the grief of the people for some of their leaders whom Herod had slain was being translated into fresh grievances against his son. Insufficient funerary honors had been offered to the Rabbis and men who had taken Herod's Roman eagle down from over the Temple gate in an act of sedition; the failure of these funerary rites was now being translated into a threat to the rite of the succession from Herod to his son.

The politicization of grief into public grievance could only be transcended by a justice that emanated from the center, that is, from Caesar himself. Only the exercise of that political will could provide the providential ordering and transcendent justice which made Caesar "the man the world most needed." The question which sociological account, the priestly or the prophetic, is more appropriate becomes an empirical question about the relation of language to reality: about whose word, so to speak, is most likely to be established. This empirical question now becomes the focus of our inquiry.

CHAPTER 2

Description, interpretation, and explanation: modes of analysis

RELIGIOUS LANGUAGE: TRANSCENDING SOCIAL BOUNDARIES AND CLOSING THE GAP BETWEEN LANGUAGE AND REALITY

It is one of the major functions of religion to anchor language in reality; Max Weber made that point years ago. Speaking of the artisan whose word was as good as gold, Weber described the Protestant Ethic as a set of beliefs and practices that anchored the promises of the artisan in the reality of conduct. No wonder that banks loaned money to the artisan; his credit was very good precisely because his words were as good as deeds. That is, the circulation of capital becomes more regular when language is rooted in reality; the resulting trust is conducive to long-term commitments in investment, accounting, and reinvestment. That is why, Weber argued, the Protestant Ethic was conducive to the spirit of capitalism.

Since this book is only an introduction to method in the sociology of religion, it would be impossible here even to try to analyze the variety of practices that enable religion to anchor language in reality. The support that religion gives to promises is only one example of the way religion undergirds language. Another is the way religion makes it possible for groups which are separated by huge barriers of property and social distance to speak to one another. Religious prophecy can help language to cross the barriers that divide the rich from the poor, the notable from the ordinary, those at the center from those on the margins of society. In providing this linguistic transcendence, as it were, religion takes speech out of the separate contexts that make it real but limited and parochial; religion thus enables language to transcend specific and concrete realities by becoming the "truth." Needless to say, this function of religion is always problematic: witness the frequent biblical references to false prophets. There are no guarantees that religion will provide this function, any more than there are assurances that evangelists will tell the truth.

To grasp the confusion and despair that corrode public life when language is not rooted in reality is one task of the sociologist of religion. I put this task first because I want the sociologist to imagine what it is like to be in a world where religion has failed to anchor speech and language itself in the bedrock of nature and society. One can grasp the functions of religion more imaginatively and intuitively if one can stand for a moment in a context where religious guarantees are both necessary and impossible. Of course, every world is presumably in need of grace: the divine gift of assurance of being in the presence of truth when all words, so to speak, have failed. My concern is with the more modest, methodological question of how one can understand what a world *with* religion is like unless one can also understand what it is like to be in the world *without* its guarantees of rooting language in reality.

It is a truism that sociologists must be able to suspend *disbelief* if they are to understand the world of another time and place. I am suggesting that it is also necessary to suspend *belief* if one is to be willing to encounter the world, as it were, on its own terms without assurances that language is grounded in reality and that the truth, therefore, is accessible. That is, method requires a certain toleration for despair. Otherwise one will not understand what religion does to make social life not only bearable but possible.

It is partly for this reason that I have chosen to use the reporting of Josephus on the first century in Palestine as I would the newspaper: that is, to introduce a world in which the relation of language to reality is problematical. The presence of despair in Josephus' world is understandable: he writes after that world has been destroyed by the Romans after the civil war of 66–70 CE and the burning of Jerusalem. Of course, there are errors and distortions in Josephus' own account. For the moment, however, it is safe enough to take his record as a slightly problematical account of words and deeds which were themselves relatively dubious or dark: an account informed not only by his biases but those of his sources, notably Nicolaus, who was also an actor and not only an observer in the accounts I have chosen to examine in this book. None the less, in Josephus' account we have a description of a world in which language is often so far removed from reality that social life itself becomes next to impossible. It is also a world in which language is often so rooted in particular contexts that transcendence through discourse of any kind becomes exceedingly difficult and yet increasingly necessary for the continuation of Herod's regime. When language is thus so difficult to establish outside the range of a few who know what is truly being said, it is very difficult to elicit the promises and commitments that a society needs from its members. That need, I will argue, becomes paramount at times of succession in the lives of individuals and of whole societies. Furthermore, the succession to the kingship left vacant by Herod was a crucial transition not only for the young man designated for the throne, Archelaus, but for the nation itself. Under these conditions it is both necessary and virtually impossible for a rite of succession to do its work. What that work really is should become more apparent as we proceed.

THE TRIAL: A FAILED ATTEMPT TO ESTABLISH THE WORD

Religion, then, has twin functions. One is to close the gap between words and deeds; the other is to enable people to communicate who are otherwise unable to transcend their own specific social categories or contexts. To illustrate these functions of religion I have chosen to focus in this chapter on a trial that took place before Caesar (Augustus) toward the end of Herod's reign (let us say the trial took place in approximately 7 BCE). Herod, for reasons that will become clearer in the course of this chapter, has reached the conclusion that two of his sons, Alexander and Aristobulus, have plans for killing him and

seizing the throne. After hearing Herod's testimony and the
defense of his sons, Caesar "urged Herod to put away all
suspicion and be reconciled to his sons," (*Antiquities* xvi.4.4;
Josephus 1969: 257). Clearly the villain of this piece is neither
Herod nor his sons but suspicion itself.

Caesar finds fault with Herod for believing the false accusations against his sons, especially "since he was unable to prove
any charge against them," and he tries to exorcise language that
is deceptive and unreliable. On the other hand, Caesar blames
the sons for arousing suspicions by failing to adopt the proper
demeanor toward their father: that is, for failing to communicate across the barriers of age and subordinate status. Caesar
requires of both sides a profound repentance, so that "such a
change of heart could not only heal the harm that had been done
to both sides but could also stimulate their good will to each
other" (*Antiquities* xvi.4.4; Josephus 1969: 257). It would be
difficult to find a more pointed assertion of the role of language
(in this case Caesar's judicial pronouncements) in managing the
succession between the generations at a time when other words
have failed both to transcend the generational barrier and to
create genuine assent in the hearts of all parties to the
generational conflict.

The scene, especially following the denunciations of the sons
by their kingly father and the sons' own tears, leads to a moment
that will remind some readers of the parable of the return of the
prodigal son. Herod's own sons kneel before him to intercede for
themselves with their father, who makes them stand up and
embraces them, "so that no one who was present, whether free
man or slave, was left unaffected" (*Antiquities* xvi.4.4; Josephus
1969: 257). That is clearly the point that Josephus is seeking to
make to the reader as well: that is, to impress them with the
grace of Caesar, who is able to utter a sentence that is superior to
the specific contexts of fathers and sons and that is effective in
deeds as well as in words of repentance. Sacred authority has
precisely that power of speech to allay suspicions, to enable
disputants to take each other at their word, to lay grievances to
rest, to effect reconciliation and the transcendence of social
differences. From a priestly perspective one should not be

surprised to find that religion restores language once more to its proper seat on the throne of reality.

From a prophetic viewpoint, however, it is not surprising to discover that even Caesar's sacred authority succeeded on this occasion only in disguising the underlying and persistent conflict over the succession to the throne. Antipater, another son (who, it will soon become apparent, was partly responsible for Herod's suspicions of his other sons), was hardly pleased at this reconciliation, since it threatened his own hopes for the succession. Josephus records that Antipater "pretended to be pleased with their reconciliation" (*Antiquities* XVI.4.5; Josephus 1969: 257). Even the two sons, whose lives had been saved by Caesar and who had been shedding tears of apparent sorrow and relief at their salvation, may still along with their supporters have experienced "considerable unrest" and "hoped for a change" (*Antiquities* XVI.4.6; Josephus 1969: 261). This awareness of the failure of sacred authority to establish the word of reconciliation is particularly interesting, since Josephus himself was writing as a member of the Flavian household, that is, under the protection of a later emperor.

Josephus was clearly biased, in his entire account, on the side of "law and order" and favored the legitimate rule of Rome over the illegitimate claims of charismatic prophets, guerilla leaders, and pretenders to the throne both in the time of Herod and during the years of the civil war. Perhaps the point here is that sacred authority is not proof against the corruption of speech by those whose hypocrisy and ambition know no bounds. However, Josephus may also have a more general interest in rooting the authority of fathers over sons in a transcendent realm of long-term commitments where all authority is conferred solely by God. Such an interest might only be implicit in this account and can be made explicit only through the sort of interpretation that an anthropologist might give of hidden meanings. I return to this subject in chapter 4.

This passage is interesting for another reason. The New Testament has numerous passages that concern the relation of sons to their fathers; indeed, several (see Mark 7:11, 13:12, 14:36) intimate that fathers had vast authority over their sons, even the power of life and death. (I have already mentioned the parable of the prodigal son.) Remember the Pauline reference to those who must have the Holy Spirit intercede for them with sighs and groans too deep for words; they must cry out "Abba," that is, "Father" (Romans 8:15). In literary form Paul's note resembles Josephus' description of the sons, who, before making their defense, were "unable to decide what to say, they were in tears and at last groaned very pitifully, for they were afraid that if they remained silent they would seem to be at a loss because of a bad conscience, while, on the other hand, they could not think up a defence because of their youth and the agitation from which they suffered" (*Antiquities* xvi.4.2; Josephus 1969: 247–249). To be overcome with tears and at a loss for words seems to be a precondition for the inspired utterances of the Spirit, whether before Caesar, "the savior of all mankind" (xvi.4.3; 1969:249), or the Father in heaven.

Above all, Josephus' point is that a kingdom divided (between fathers and sons and thus) against itself cannot stand: a point that will seem familiar to readers of Jesus' later arguments with the Pharisees over his own sources of authority and inspiration. It is thus vital for the survival and continuity of the nation that the conflict between the generations be healed. To overcome that conflict, however, it is first necessary to allay suspicions, and to do that requires an institution that will establish the word, that is, provide an account of what in fact prevails between the generations: one that is not open to contradiction and is therefore as persuasive as it is authoritative.

Thus there is a fearful symmetry between the task of the trial and that of the sociologist. Both seek to arrive at an authoritative description of what has happened, long before either attempts to make an interpretation, to explain the course of events or to pass judgment on the actors involved. To allay suspicion is the task of every author and of authority itself in establishing an incontrovertible account. The problems of arriving at such an authoritative description are the subject of this chapter.

DESCRIPTION: LOOKING FOR SOCIAL FACTS

The first task of the sociologist, then, is to describe the social facts that come into play in the specific situation. By "social facts" I mean the basic building blocks of social life; they are the fundamental structure of society, like the cells of the body. They are beyond actions; in fact they are actions that have been construed or can become construed into *acts*: acts of compassion or self-sacrifice, for instance; acts of folly or courage; or, more formally, acts in the economic sphere, or in the sphere of the sacred, where one appeals to those in authority or claims access to extraordinary, even supernatural, sources of inspiration. I will have more to say on the subject of acts as the basic set of social facts later in this chapter. Here I wish simply to point out how hard it is to know an act for what it is.

The sociologist and the citizen start out, then, in precisely the same posture of inquiry. Both want to know whether a particular action, for instance, is an act of negligence or homicide, whether they are serving on a jury, bringing suit, reading, or watching the nightly news on television. Indeed, that is why societies have trials and liturgies: i.e. to resolve any residual questions as to what sort of act a particular action really is. As Runciman puts it, the job of the sociologist is at the outset simply to present a set of "social facts on the reportage of whose occurrence rival observers can agree" (1989: 9).

Of course, the task is seldom simple, except when all has been said or done to construe an action into an act, for example, when a minister pronounces a couple to be duly married or the Speaker of the House announces an act of Congress to have been completed. Whether the marriage is a good one or the act of Congress wise can be debated at some length for quite a long time. That, however, is a matter of interpretation, and I will try to suggest the differences between describing and interpreting or evaluating later in this chapter. Here it is enough to point out the difficulty in knowing whether an action is, for instance, an act of sedition, a form of legitimate protest, or even an act of insanity. Certainly dissidents in Soviet Russia have had at times to keep the debate alive as to whether they are engaging in sedition, legitimate protest, or a display of mental illness. To construe an action as a social act is problematic, then, not only because there are problems of interpretation, but because any definition may include a covert explanation for what has been said and done. To define social protest as mental illness is to preempt discussion with an official explanation. I will also try to be somewhat clearer on the difference between describing, or interpreting, and actually explaining social facts later in this same chapter.

If anyone were in doubt about how contentious is the job of describing actions as social facts, that is, as acts of one kind or another, Josephus' account of the fate of Aristobulus and Alexander should be helpful in allaying such doubt. In fact, that is one reason I have chosen to begin with this chapter from Josephus. Consider how problematical were the reports of what Aristobulus and Alexander were actually saying. Josephus makes it clear that, when these two sons returned to Jerusalem after their mother's murder, they were resentful of their father and spoke often about their mother; indeed, "The youths too, on their part, were rather reckless and were hostile to their father both because of their remembrance of their mother's undeserved fate and also because of their desire to rule" (*Antiquities* XVI.3.1; Josephus 1969: 233). Josephus is at some pains to describe the young men as open, forthright, even too bold for their own good, but as unskilled in the subtleties of palace intrigue as they were in the arts of defence at their later trial before Caesar. (There may, then, be some bias in the reporting on the basis of which I am trying to arrive at this description of social acts, but that is a matter for later discussion.) Salome, however, with Herod's brother, Pheroras, "showed malice toward the youths and formed elaborate plots against them" (*Antiquities* XVI.3.1; Josephus 1969: 235). She was spiteful, because she wanted, Josephus suggests, to make sure that none of Mariamme's sons might live to take revenge for their mother's murder. As for Salome's subtlety, it consisted of spreading rumors that the sons "were far from pleased to be with their father because of the death of their mother," hinting that they might rather be rid of him (*Antiquities* XVI.1.2; Josephus 1969: 211). Salome and her co-conspirators were clearly hinting that the sons would like to be rid of their father. The hint was not lost on Herod.

Other conversations, equally subtle and deceptive, added to the ambiguity. Antipater's contributions to the lies and distortions of the truth made the other sons' actions very hard to construe into well-defined social acts. Antipater, of course, was another son of Herod's, whom Herod had brought forward to deflate his other two sons' pretensions to the throne. Like Salome, Antipater took what the other sons actually were saying and had it reported "in exaggerated form" to Herod; even more subtle was Antipater's use of otherwise trustworthy and apparently disinterested individuals to be the bearers of the bad news to Herod (*Antiquities* xvi.3.3; 1969: 241). The result, therefore, was a thorough confusion not only of Herod's but of the public's understanding of the nature of the sons' actions. Were they the acts of grief, of foolhardy youthful protest, or of rebellion and sedition? This problematic is the same for the sociological observer, of course, as it was for the participants themselves.

It is also a problematic to which the Synoptic Gospels are addressed in their attention to public discussion of Jesus as the son of Joseph and Mary, of David, or even of God (see Luke 2:48–49, 14:26, 15:11–32; Mark 3:31–35). Was he foolhardy, seditious, or righteous? Certainly one way to read the Synoptics is as an account of attempts during Jesus' lifetime to determine the nature of his deeds, since the same actions could be construed as acts of mercy or of offense against the law. The Synoptics themselves, of course, are also attempts at reconstruction of his actions into acts of redemption, salvation, or of whatever category the gospel writers adopted for the purpose. Thus for the sociologist the task of describing actions that are construed into acts faces the same pitfalls as were encountered by the people originally involved in the social life being investigated: not to mention the pitfalls imposed by the passage of time, the difference in contexts, and the opacity of the texts themselves.

Any confusion in describing social actions poses a real threat to the existence of society, precisely because acts are the basic units of social structure. Sociologically speaking, it is a confusion in the relation of language to reality, and that relation which is fundamental to the construction of acts out of actions. Actions seldom, if ever, speak for themselves. It takes words, and sometimes extended discourse or even litigation, to turn trouble-some actions into acts "on the reportage of whose occurrence rival observers can agree," as Runciman put it in the quotation given earlier. In Josephus' account, the observers were slaves and freedmen, officers in the military and office-holders in Herod's administration, as well as members of the family who were taking various sides in the conflict among the brothers and between them and their father. The observers were also, however, in the streets and the market-place. Josephus notes that "the whole city was filled with talk about these things" (*Antiquities* xvi.3.1; Josephus 1969: 235). This means, therefore, that the city itself was uncertain about the fundamental link between language and reality, because it could not agree on how to construe the actions of the sons into acts of one kind or another.

Lest any reader think that this interpretation of the situation is too extreme, consider Josephus' term for what it meant to bring these rumors to the attention of Caesar himself: Herod thought it necessary "to reveal to Caesar" his sons' alleged conspiracy and "to *pollute* his ears with such a recital" (*Antiquities* xvi.4.1; Josephus 1969: 245; my italics). Pollution destroys the vitality and wholeness of the social order; the separation of language from reality opens up a serious gap that is threatening to the life of the society itself: threatening in the same way that pollution may poison the wells of discourse which contain the life-giving waters of the *polis*. One can therefore imagine the intense public demand for a teacher or prophet whose words would be incontrovertible, as good as deeds (see Luke 4:21, 5:24, 6:46–49, 7:8–9, 7:22, 11:28; Mark 4:40–41, 9:29).

INTERPRETATION

With these comments, however, I have shifted from description to what I will call interpretation. By linking together Josephus' observations about rumors with his statements about the pollution caused by deceptive, ambiguous, or controversial language, I am beginning to show how various separate observations may actually hang together. It is the task of interpretation to transcend partial, particular, or common sense. Description seeks to arrive at a reliable sense of what acts are being performed by individuals who are engaged in a set of actions, that is, to decipher and evaluate the rumors and accusations surrounding the sons of Herod. To ask *what it was like* to experience this confusion, however, is to make another sort of sense of these unhappy proceedings. That larger sense concerns the intentions of people; that is why Salome's desire to prevent the sons from avenging their mother's death is important for interpreting as well as for describing the acts of the sons themselves.

More than acknowledgment of intentions is at stake, however, when the analysis shifts to interpretation. As I have mentioned, here it becomes important to look for correlates of the act in question: for instance, the confusion of discourse in the streets and the impurity of the language that is spoken even before Caesar himself. It is only by looking at the correlates of social acts that we can begin to know what it was like to live in a world where language had at best a problematical relation to reality. It was like living, Josephus seems to suggest, in a world where impurities were present in the wells of the city. The life of the city, even of the whole society, was being threatened by impure discourse. Remember, in this connection, the close attention paid by the Pharisees and Herodian spies to the words of Jesus, his conversations with the disciples, and his public messages. Where there is even a hint that someone is claiming the right of succession to a position of authority, not to mention kingship, a society will pay the closest attention to the meaning of words, to the nature of social actions as acts, and to the pretender's sources of inspiration and authority.

INTERPRETATION AND CONTEXT: FROM HEROD'S SOLACE TO CAESAR'S

In Josephus' account of this episode between Herod, his sons, and Caesar, a number of actions stand out as something more than behavior: they seem practiced, as though they were part of

a play or even a liturgy. Take, for example, Alexander's speech
(and his brother's) in his defense. Some might look at the speech
for its rhetorical qualities; no doubt he follows the patterns of
rhetoric for persuasive speech that he had learned earlier as a
student in Rome. Cicero might have been pleased with his use of
rhetorical questions, of hypothetical statements, and disclaimers
against making defense, since "acts which have not been
committed do not admit of any defence" (*Antiquities* xvi.3.3;
Josephus 1969: 253). The sociologist, however, looks for signs
that the speaker is engaged in a familiar act that is constituted by
these linguistic strategies. Alexander's speech is indeed an
"apology": an apologia in the classical sense of an extended
defense and explanation. It is one form of speech that seeks to
transcend the barriers of subordinate social status: of age,
gender, and imputed guilt.

The context helps to identify Alexander's actions even
further; noting that the hearing before Caesar is in fact a "trial,"
Alexander goes on to refer to Caesar as a "witness." Caesar,
however, is not merely a jury; he is also "the saviour of all
mankind" and "the lord of all men and our mediator at the
present moment" (*Antiquities* xvi.3.3; Josephus 1969: 249, 253).
Alexander is therefore engaging in an act of the most serious
nature: testimony on his own behalf before the final arbiter of
human destiny in the known world. This is an "apologia" for his
entire life, and he claims to be ready therefore to forfeit his life if
the defense, his own apologia, fails. In case the seriousness of his
speech is missed, he reminds us that being brought before Caesar
is like being brought to the altar in the sanctuary: a place where
no man can be slaughtered before the bar of ultimate judgment.
This is the most serious act of speech, then, in which a man can
engage: an apologia before the final witness and only mediator,
Caesar, who is also the judge in the court of last appeal on this
earth. Caesar's sentence is beyond doubt or cavil; it is, quite
literally, the last word. Does Caesar's final word of judgment
also act as a type of authority in New Testament discussions of
the last judgment?

Identifying such an act places the sociologist at the beginning
of the search for an adequate account. At the very beginning one

needs more than a little bit of behavior or gesture: something more permanent or, as sociologists often put it, more "institutionalized." To be institutionalized means that an action is really a practice: something that individuals are likely to do, in specific situations, along fairly conventional lines. Borrowing a term from the theater, a sociologist would call such a practice a "role": a part in the play of social life. To be in a role one needs to know what is expected: what to say, how to present oneself, how to begin and how to end. It is just as necessary for a patient in the doctor's office to know the role of being a patient as it was for Alexander to know how to speak in his own defense at the trial before Caesar. Sometimes one's life can depend on one's role-taking or role-playing abilities.

Many sociologists think of roles as basic to societies in the way that cells are basic to tissues in a living body. In this introduction to the sociology of religion, however, I am not going to take roles as the basic unit of social life; I am arguing that it is preferable to think of the "act" as more basic than the "role," since every role is in fact likely to be based on a number of acts. In his role as defendant Alexander engages in the act of making an apologia; he also, however, engages in weeping when rendered (temporarily) speechless, and later engages in an act of "intercession" with his father Herod by falling down on his knees before him. As the prodigal son (Luke 15:11–32) returning to the father also fell on his knees, such an act was clearly not confined to the courtroom but was a rhetorical strategy typical of sons seeking "intercession" with their fathers. One act at a time, so to speak, will be more than enough for starting out on a sociological analysis.

This rather piecemeal approach may seem very frustrating to anyone who has sensed the tragedy and the drama, not to mention the anguish, in the conflict between Herod and his sons. Certainly an introductory course in sociology can permanently maim or destroy whatever fledgling interest the student may have had, as the instructor intones the necessity for careful use of terms such as role, role-taking, role-playing, and so on. The student may rightfully demand to know what all that has to do with the frightening power – in the case of Herod – that a

Roman father had over his sons: for example, the power to destroy. A demand to get on with the story might insist on raising the specter of the dead Mariamme, which haunts her two sons when they return after her murder. What about the malicious gossip of Salome, who poisoned the discourse of the court and even of the city of Jerusalem with her rumors? Isn't this story about tyrants, ambitious or seditious women, sub-verted followers, credulous publics? Yes, but it is also about the relation of patriarchs to patrimony, about crises of succession, about the separation of words from deeds and of actions from socially constructed acts; no wonder, then, that it is also about a kingdom so divided by such contradictions that it eventually fell.

That is why a sociological account will also need to examine the widening gap between social institutions and speech: the presence of distortions, lies, secrets, rumors, and the eventual failure of language to be based in reality. The account will not be done, furthermore, until a word has been spoken about the relation of power to misery; that relationship is not quite as simple as it seems to those who associate being miserable with being powerless. What we need, then, is a way of analyzing social life that will lead us into each of the problems in some sort of logical order: a method that will also make us sensitive to the shift from reporting things to interpreting, or explaining, or evaluating them (Runciman 1983). That is why I find it necessary to begin with the relatively obvious and simple before going on to the inevitable complexities of the analysis.

The act of making an apologia, of speaking in one's own defense before the one who has the authority to dispose of one's case or even to dispose of oneself, is one of several acts that have to do with addressing those in authority. There are other acts such as appeals and intercessions; Josephus notes many of them in the course of his account of the history and the wars of the Jewish people. In fact, it is tempting to suggest that this is what Josephus was all about: that is, recording the various ways in which individuals, groups, or the representatives of an entire people approached and addressed those in authority over them. For lack of a better word, I will call this class of acts the "sacred," because they involve asymmetrical, diffuse, long-term obligations.

Of course, there are other classes of acts, many of which also appear in Josephus: secular acts that were quite common in antiquity. Runciman mentions, for instance, that

The basis of the twentieth-century researcher's account of the ancient Roman economy rests on the evidence of his sources for *acts of* buying and selling, borrowing and lending, mortgaging and foreclosing, hoarding, taxing, bequeathing, etc., which taken together constitute the "economy" about which he writes. (1983: 14; my italics)

These acts entail symmetrical, specific, and relatively short-term obligations. Runciman goes on to suggest that this classification of acts belonging to an economy might seem surprising to a Roman, but that that is quite all right; observers have another perspective, which may be an improvement on that of the actors themselves. As I will argue in chapter 4, observers have a right to their own ways of seeing things. In any event, anyone, let alone someone like myself arriving two thousands years too late on the scene, will provide only a problematical account of the acts in question. Even the New Testament is a problematical *report* on the acts that made up the sacred, in the sense of stating what happened when, where, to whom, and in what order, and it testifies to the political and apologetic aspects of reports on the activities of Jesus even in his lifetime.

The task of *interpreting* what it was like to engage in sacred acts will be a more difficult one. By that I mean something more than understanding the moods, the motives, the needs, and the aspirations of individuals addressing the authorities in their lives. I mean also what it was like to be in a world where the authorities could dispose of one so thoroughly as, for instance, fathers could dispose of their sons. (Runciman calls *this* the task of description, as compared to "reporting." To make it clear how much is at stake in such a process, however, I prefer to use the term interpretation.)

It is grasping the way-things-hang-together, I am suggesting, that makes an interpretation more than a simple account of motives and goals, beliefs and values. Weber was attempting to interpret the Protestant Ethic in this fashion by showing how it was part of a larger constellation of acts associated with time and money, symbols and speech. And he understood some such pattern to be essential for any society that included the sacred. I would like to approach the acts of addressing authority in the same way, that is, as part of a constellation – some might call it a pattern – by which language is rooted in social reality and yet not only reproduces but shapes that reality. When speech, especially sacred forms of address, challenges social reality, the sociological analogue to what theologians mean by revelation may be at hand.

If that seems unnecessarily dramatic, think for a moment about the trial of the sons of Herod before Caesar: it did have its dramatic aspects. By that I mean to refer to something more than the theatricals of apologia and accusation that we have just been examining. What the drama reveals, I would suggest, is what it is like to live within a society where fathers have virtually unlimited power over sons because they depend on those sons for the continuity of patrilineal succession. Indeed, sons have much to gain from their father's death, for instance, access to the father's position, wealth, and power, whether it is a small family business, a farm, or the throne of Herod. Just as they have much to gain from the succession, then, they have much to fear from their father's anger: especially from the anger of a father like Herod, who suspects his sons of being prematurely eager to succeed him. A certain paternal paranoia is understandable, perhaps inevitable, in any patriarchal society that is also patrilineal; to this structurally induced paranoia, of course, Herod added his own fearful suspicions. What is dramatized in this trial, then, is partly a form of paranoia, mixed with the yearnings of father and son for access to one another, that life may go on, regardless of the larger issues of succession to the kingship itself.

The dramatic aspect of the trial, then, may suggest some questions for the New Testament scholar to pursue. If the trial is revelatory in some sense, it is possible that the same paranoia and hope could affect the relation of fathers to sons elsewhere in Palestinian society. There may have been a yearning for reconciliation between fathers and sons, of the sort that Jesus expressed in the parable of the two sons (Luke 15:11–32). There may also have been a very heavy weight of obligation binding sons to fathers: sons who must pay the proper funerary respects, or tend the nets of their fathers' fishing boats, or till ancestral land to save the family farm. The nonpayment of these dues could become a source of considerable dread: far more serious, in a psychological sense, than the dread of official punishment for the failure to pay proper tithes or taxes, although these obligations also weighed heavily on Jewish males of the period. The trial, then, dramatizes a mixture of dread and despair that may have been far more common than the circumstances of this story would suggest.

It is the mixture of these conflicting emotions that is particularly revelatory, I would argue. In order to avoid the father's anger and a possible death sentence, the sons must lower their aspirations and lead a relatively circumscribed life: as Caesar Augustus reminded them, it was their lack of submissive demeanor that may have aroused their father's suspicions. On the other hand, in laying hold on the succession in due time, through the grace of a father to whom they are reconciled, they are also recognizing that the time will come for them as well to renounce their throne and to yield it to another generation. The gift of the succession comes with a price: it will eventually have to be relinquished, like life itself. The trial therefore reveals a double-bind, in which to avoid the threat of death sons must lead circumscribed lives, while to embrace the full rights of succession to paternal authority, they must be willing in turn to surrender that authority to their sons and to undergo, at least symbolically and socially, a ritualized form of death. A compromise with death diminishes one's life, but a full measure of life's rewards must be paid for in the end.

What is revealed, then, in this drama is a dilemma which may be endemic to social life or may merely have been particularly widespread in a patrilineal and patriarchal society such as pre-70 CE Palestine, in which the rights of sons *vis-à-vis* their fathers may have been a focus of intense conflict within and between the generations. Whether that conflict could be found outside the Palestine of the period is an important comparative question, but it is outside the immediate scope of this introductory essay on method.

The interpretive task is still before us, furthermore, and in that connection I have one further question to raise. It concerns the use of trials to dramatize a society's sense of what makes for good and evil. Clearly in this trial whatever sustains the succession from father to son is "good";[1] and the authority of Caesar is of paramount significance in laying to rest the antagonism between the generations that threatened the Herodian succession with an irreversible disruption and tragedy. Latent, beneath the manifest significance of the trial, however, lies another meaning that is only hinted at rather than revealed. It concerns the nature of evil.

At some point, it is tempting to move quickly from interpretation to evaluation. Especially when issues of what makes a "good" father have come to trial in a narrative history, it will seem necessary to consider the text's own evaluation of good and evil, even if only as a prelude to passing a modern verdict on the trial. If Caesar is a good ruler, that is, the prototypical good father, it is possible that Josephus' drama is meant to suggest that there is an element of evil in the fact that Herod even brought his sons to trial. Herod, as later narratives will make even more apparent, chafed at the terms of the double-bind that I have just described. Willing to receive the succession from Caesar, he was clearly loath to relinquish his powers to his sons. Unwilling to compromise with death by adopting a limited life-style and modest prerogatives, he provoked the threat of death from enemies that he made by his virtually unlimited

---

[1] There is an important distinction here between modern and classical notions of a "good" father, and there is also an important distinction between these latter, antique notions of good fatherhood and the good that is the opposite of the evil stemming from an interrupted succession between the generations. First, concerning the classical notion of what makes for a good father, consider Veyne's comment that in classical Rome "Only severity, which terrifies appetites susceptible to temptation, can give strength of character ... Severity was part of the father's role; the mother pleaded for leniency" (1987: 16). More important, then, than an apparently (by modern standards) "good" relation between fathers and sons was the maintenance of the succession. As Veyne puts it, "Tenderness was misplaced. But it was legitimate to mourn the ruin of a family's hopes" (1987: 17).

grasp of wealth and power. Is this trial, then, meant to dramatize the encounter between good and evil? Or do we have here mainly the literary expression of Josephus' respect for Caesar and his palpable disgust with Herod? The relation of this text to the society of its time is problematical, of course. None the less, I will argue in a later chapter that the concept of evil is essential for our understanding of what it is like to experience a threat to a society's ability to reproduce itself. More specifically, evil is seen as a threat to the tissue of obligation that binds together the living with the dead and one generation to another. Even that use of the concept of evil, however, stays within the realm of interpretation and does not take the leap to evaluating the events of the trial itself. Whether or not the sociologist ever takes up the cudgels of evaluation, however, a prior task remains: the problem of explanation.

EXPLANATION

The task of interpretation is open-ended. To show what it is like to live in a world where language cannot be counted on to reflect or create social reality, we must ask why the trial before Caesar failed to close that gap once and for all. Of course, words of contrition and reconciliation were spoken by Herod and his sons, after Caesar had pronounced his own judgment in the known world's court of last appeal. None the less, the three brothers continued to conspire and to contemplate making "innovations"; Antipater, whose interest in the succession had become threatened by the apparent reconciliation of his father to Alexander and Aristobulus, apparently masked his resentment under a show of contentment while continuing to plan for his own eventual triumph. It would not be unlikely for Herod therefore to fall back on another ritual, or additional drama, in order to repair the breach between language and reality.

Power is not a seamless garment, worn by those who have it and envied by those who do not. Runciman (1989) notes that it is woven of several strands, notably control over economic resources, over military and other forms of coercion, and, finally, over ideological resources for "persuasion." Even within one such strand, however, there are often loose threads. For instance, powers of persuasion are often vested in individuals by virtue of their family background, their ethnic status, their rights to perform or to engage in certain rituals, and their control over the means of education or communication, to name only a few (Runciman 1989: 23–24). Consider the current rulers of China, for instance, who seek to control not only the market and the factories as well as the military but also the mass media and the universities. Even within their ranks, however, the various dimensions of power are not evenly and equally possessed. Control over the armies, for instance, depends partly on kinship: witness the different degrees of loyalty and dissent between the 37th Army, which took Tiananmen Square from the people, and the armies that remained on the outskirts or actually refused to engage in the repression. Family loyalties were expressed as divisions within the military.

Runciman's point goes even further, however, in locating internal weakness within the fabric of social power. He finds that even within the "ideological" dimension, an individual may be strong, for instance, with regard to family but weak in another regard, for example, his or her ethnic background or right to appear in places of honor at ceremonial functions.[2] It is authority that can close the gap between what is said and what is done, that is, between language and reality, but authority does little to close that gap when it holds uneven or inconsistent threads of social power in its hands.

In ritual the last word is supposedly spoken, and all is both said and done to close the gap between language and reality. Rituals, however, are known to fail. The trial before Caesar is a

---

[2] An inscription at Narbo, "of uncertain date" but probably in the Augustan era, describes the ceremonial prerogatives of a *flamen* who "performs the rite and offers sacrifice: " "let him have the right to watch the public games of that province, seated among the decurions or senators on the first bench . . . the wife of the flamen dressed in white or purple on festival days . . . let her not swear an oath against her will nor touch the body of a dead man . . . unless that man is a relative" (Braund 1985: 65). Note how the ceremonial attributes of power and authority extend to the wife of the *flamen*, but note also how that derived power comes with the obligation to preserve speech that is authentic (not swearing an oath against her will). Note finally that such speech is associated with purity, since the wife is also enjoined from engaging in other (nonlinguistic) acts that might pollute the *polis*, such as touching a dead body.

case in point: not an isolated or extreme case. In his study of a funeral in Java, for instance, Clifford Geertz (1989) noted that the rite was subject to an excruciating delay while the parties sought to resolve the tension created by a discrepancy in the status of the officiant: as the mayor, the officiant had the right and obligation to perform the funeral of the boy, but as a member of an opposing ethnic group he was unacceptable to the bereaved family. As the day dragged on, and the boy's body lay under the sun, the tension mounted until the boy's father gave what was for the Javanese a most unusual speech about his own feelings in the matter. The barriers between social groups may be used to symbolize good and evil; when ritual fails, these sources of opposition may not be transcended by the usual pronouncements of those in authority. Under these conditions the barriers may become so intolerable that they are overcome only by inspired speech or, when words fail, by hard actions. Note that there is a familiar constellation of factors in this account: the possibility of pollution by death, the pollution of public discourse by speech filled with suspicion, language that is not adequate to manage the succession from one status (the living) to the next (the dead), and authority that is prevented by ethnic and religious divisions from being given popular acceptance. Under these conditions, one can accept innovations in religious belief as public speech as well as the breakdown of ritual into more chaotic and perhaps abusive public demonstrations.

Now, think once again about the various threads of power that were lying ready to hand for the sons of Herod. As sons they were clearly in the line of succession until Herod brought forward another son, Antipater, to "depress" their pretensions; kinship itself therefore provided them with an ambiguous connection to the succession. (As sons of Mariamme they enjoyed the same sort of ambiguous status: her ethnicity itself putting them at a disadvantage in the eyes of some, like Salome, whose loyalties were entirely Idumaean rather than Hasmonean.) As members of the younger generation the sons enjoyed considerable popularity among the people and at least the benefit of the doubt among some members of Herod's household; for others their age was a cause for suspicion because it made them part of an age-set, youth, that was perennially seeking power. All these distinctions, I should add, are entirely within what Runciman calls the "ideological" aspects of social power: they concern the powers of persuasion and the chances of being taken at one's word. In fact, Runciman (1989: 23–24) mentions age-set, status-group, and faction along with caste as customary sources of confusion in the ideological dimension of power, because a person may rank high in one regard and low in another. The problem of being taken seriously, then, is compounded because some have the power to construe others' actions into acts. That power is exercised ideologically, furthermore, when those who can construe actions into acts code perennial forms of opposition, for example, between generations and gender-groups, in terms of the symbolic opposition between life and death or good and evil.[3]

In describing the situation that led to the trial, along with the trial itself, our task was essentially the same as the task of Caesar at the sons' trial: that is, to construe certain actions of theirs into acts (of sedition, immaturity, loyalty, ambition, and so forth). Both the sociologist and the trial judge have to construe ambiguous and problematical actions into acts on the nature of which rival observers can agree. That is extremely difficult when only sociologists' language has to be taken into account; the relation of typical concepts like "alienation" or "class" to social reality remains problematic no matter how many Ph.D. dissertations have been spawned in the process of seeking clarification. How much more difficult it is to arrive at a satisfactory description of the facts when the world one is describing is itself plagued by a chronic, sometimes acute, disturbance in the relation of language to reality. When it comes to interpreting actions as acts, moreover, both the sociologist and the judge have to take into account seemingly unrelated

---

[3] According to Paul Veyne (1987: 28–29), no matter how noble a son's lineage, sons under Roman law had no legal rights and could not engage in contracts, leave legacies, free slaves, or even have a career without their fathers' consent; they thus resembled slaves in status and power, and like slaves could be put to death by their fathers. Veyne notes, however, that "the youth's father was his natural judge and could privately sentence him to death" (1987: 27).

events: conversations, patterns of behavior, gestures, previous occurrences of hostility or fidelity, and so forth. The constellation of relevant events is difficult to define; that is why judges and sociologists alike have to define what is relevant in the way of evidence: a difficult task at best, when one does not yet have a theory to work with, but only a problem-area. It is even more difficult when, as in our case, the problem-area itself concerns the ambiguous relation of words to deeds and of speech to social action. As part of the task of interpretation, we went on to ask, "What is it like to live in a world in which language is not firmly rooted or expressed in reality?" Our answer led us to focus on a certain chronic suspicion or paranoia in the relation of fathers to sons. When we began to argue that such paranoia seemed to be structurally induced by the facts of patriarchy in a patrilineal society, we had begun to explain the trial and its surrounding events rather than merely to interpret them. Our mode of analysis first shifted from description to interpretation; now our mode of analysis shifts to explanation. In the move from interpreting the relation of language to reality to explaining it, we have begun to focus not on the way-things-hang-together but on the conditions that give rise to the problematic relation of language to reality. No longer asking, "What is it like?," we are asking "How – really why – did it happen?"

As sociologists, we are really asking for the answer to this question: "*Under what conditions* does language depart from reality in such a way that it becomes difficult finally to construe certain actions (for example, those of Herod and his sons) into acts?" Explanation brings description and interpretation to the point at which we can imagine how the world we are examining could have been otherwise, because we begin to know the conditions under which the world we are examining actually developed. To know how it could be otherwise, furthermore, opens up the possibility for what Runciman calls "evaluation": the discussion of alternative worlds. That is to get well ahead of this early stage in the development of a method for engaging in the sociology of religion; besides, there is something more to be said for the moment about explanation itself.

It is important to be very modest about what one is

attempting to explain, because within every explanation there are terms which themselves are problematical, require interpretation, and could become what-is-to-be-explained themselves. Take, for example, our attempt to explain why a ritual, such as the trial before Caesar, did not resolve all doubts about what sort of acts the sons and their father were engaging in. Some of the conditions which made the failure of the trial possible, if not inevitable, were "given": that is, part of what was built into the situation. There were inconsistencies between various aspects of the role of son-of-Herod; for instance, the sons were both wards of Caesar and yet subject to their father's domination. As Runciman points out, a role in a hierarchy of status "may at the same time be a function of relations of domination either external to the society or internal to a sub-system within it" (1989: 18). That is, the son-of-Herod was also related to a chain of authority and power that led outside of Herod's kingdom to the throne of Caesar; the son-of-Herod was also a member of such other subsystems, outside the family, as their ethnic group and the world of public opinion. It may be possible to explain the uncertainty about the relation of their actions to well-known, clearly defined acts (for example, whether to construe them as acts of loyalty, of impetuous youth, or of subversion) by referring to the discrepancies in aspects of their roles. The conflict between paternal and Caesarian authority could also help us to account for why the trial had more apparent than real success.

This attention to structural sources of opposition recalls the work of Bloch and his associates discussed in chapter 1. Our problem is to explain Palestinian – and particularly Herodian – preoccupation with certain structural sources of opposition: especially opposition between fathers and sons, men and women, Rome and Jerusalem. The question is whether these sources of tension and contradiction *caused* the social dramas (which then attempted to relieve and transcend the conflicts between genders or generations); or whether, on the other hand, the trial was itself an attempt to dramatize the society's ability to create a social order in which these contradictions no longer appeared. In the latter case, then, it would have been necessary to invent the tensions between generations in order to have the ritualized display of Caesar's authoritative power to transform and dissolve them in a symbolic victory over the forces of decay, death, and destruction. As Bloch seemed to suggest, a society that considers its social order to be providential if not divine must reassure itself that it has achieved a fusion of such opposites as birth and death. That is why, perhaps, the sight of father and sons embracing at this trial was so moving. If the threat were not real, it would have had to be created for the symbolic victory over inter-generational opposition to take place.

As a sociologist, however, one cannot be content with one theory as a guide to research: one needs an alternative explanation in order to prevent merely circular thinking. As an alternative to this structural explanation, therefore, I would suggest that one consider psychoanalytic theory, which finds it necessary to consider motives and intentions – some of which are conscious, but many of which are certainly not. To engage in a ritual may permit some of these motives and intentions to be expressed; certainly it was necessary for there to have been an element of confession in Alexander's passionate apologia. What were confessed, however, were not the Oedipal strivings of a son deprived of his mother and hell-bent on eliminating the rival father; only the best of filial sentiments were acknowledged in that speech. Rituals do have a way of claiming to be more revealing than they are; aggressions deep in the human heart can hide behind matter-of-fact confessions of contrition for having missed opportunities and for having caused harm to one's fellow human beings. Whenever such serious and lengthy speech pours forth from a dutiful son, however, it may well be that parricidal emotions are indeed hiding within the rite of reconciliation.

The private inspiration behind public testimony, whether in the churches' liturgies or the trials of the state, may therefore be unsuitable for expression. Psychoanalytic theory, of course, would be able to find several possible reasons for Alexander's claim that he could find no "real evidence" of conspiracy either in his own actions or in his heart. Josephus was not convinced, and perhaps neither was Antipater nor Herod himself, as the remainder of Josephus' account of this family feud makes very clear. Until public authority and private inspiration can be combined in a single role, however, there will always remain reasonable doubt about the relation of speech to deeds and of acts to actions. Under these conditions whoever reigns may be unable to rule, whether it be Herod the king of the Jews or King Minos of Crete. Faith will then find other objects of devotion where the unity of authority and inspiration is more believable. Those objects of devotion may be on the periphery of a society, especially when the rites of the center have failed to carry conviction and create devotion. When the rituals of the center fail to provide either a sufficient or a final word, those who claim extraordinary sources of inspiration and authority will seek to establish the word on their own initiative.

CHAPTER 3

Levels of observation and of analysis: making the right choices

REVIEWING THE ARGUMENT: THE DIFFICULT TASK OF INTERPRETATION

We have been engaged in several preliminary reflections on the tensions in Palestinian society at the time of the death of Herod. On the one hand, the trial of the sons of Herod before Caesar suggests that there was a rising popular as well as political demand to resolve the controversy between generations not only in that household, I have argued, but in the society itself. What makes this demand "serious," furthermore, is what commends it to the attention of a sociologist of religion. It is "la vie sérieuse," as Durkheim put it, that constitutes the province of the sociologist of religion: not merely the groups and movements, institutions or major figures that are conventionally defined as "religious." Now, in the conflict between generations, far more is at stake than the survival of the Herodian regime or the honors for the dead demanded by the followers of slain Rabbis. In according these honors the nation achieves its own line of spiritual succession and guarantees, as it were, its own continuity and vitality. Those honors conflicted, quite clearly, with the honors demanded by Archelaus at the moment of his succession. In the stalemate between the two lines of succession, the life of the nation itself is at stake. The two social systems, one Roman and the other national, have thus reached a stand-off that threatens the survival of both of them. At such times there is inevitably a demand for a final, authoritative word that will resolve the stalemate and allow life to go on.

It is one thing to *explain* the stalemate between the generations, perhaps by evoking a theory of the way individuals had to live simultaneously within two contradictory but overlapping social systems, the one imperial and the other a proud and sacred nation. It is quite another to *understand* what it was like to live under these conditions. In the explanatory mode of analysis, I have pointed to the threat of imperial or regal resolution of the controversy; other threats, whether of filicide, parricide, assassination, execution, or revolt, as well as of renewed oppression, were also hanging over the nation. In the interpretive mode of analysis, I have pointed to unfulfilled longings for reconciliation between generations and for the continued blessing of the dead, the desire for access to the kingship, suspicion and paranoia, and dread of retribution for regicidal thoughts and regal ambitions. Throughout, however, our attention has remained on the problematical relation of words and gestures to social reality. For instance, Herod's sons' attempt to forestall suspicion and ward off their father's anger required, if Caesar's judgment was correct, a modest demeanor, close attention to what was said, and the corresponding constraints on their ambitions and wishes. To forestall the threat of a parental judgment which could be fatal, it is necessary to live a diminished life.

Under these conditions, I am suggesting, demand arises for a word of revelation: a final sentence that will resolve the stalemate, renew and guarantee the life of the nation, and postpone the final conflict, whether between nation and empire or between fathers and sons. To put it another way, these social dramas, serious as they are, set the stage for dramas of salvation in which the implicit themes become explicit and the sacred aspects of social life appear in their religious dimensions. Under these conditions, I am suggesting, the slippery relationship of language to social life becomes intolerable, and the demand for closure through authoritative speech becomes intense, if not entirely irresistible.

Needless to say, we already have a methodological tiger by the proverbial tail. To put it simply, it is no easy thing to investigate speech that may well be deceptive and hypocritical. Take, for example, a recent study of the way Chinese businessmen conduct themselves. Far removed from our immediate concerns, it illustrates several methodological problems. According to one investigator, Linda Wei Ling Young (1982), these businessmen seem to Americans to be devious, deferential, and even "downright inept." That is because the Chinese rhetorical strategy leaves the "punch line," the request or proposal, until the end; it comes after the speaker's preliminary comments have given others an idea of the problem and of the speaker's resources or interests. Equally crucial is the speaker's apparent willingness to take others into account without putting himself or herself forward or presuming on others' good-will and consent. Ms. Young goes on to argue that deviousness is therefore in the eye of the beholder: what Americans see as "beating around the bush" is a Chinese strategy for building consent and legitimacy through an "avalanche of relevant details" put forward without any risk that the speaker will be seen as "rude" or "pushy" (1982: 79–80).

I mention this to suggest that there are differences between actors and observers that can produce serious distortions in viewpoint: what appears to the observer as deviousness, Young (1982) points out, may well be a cultural difference in ways of building an argument. Not all distortions are due to cultural differences, of course. Other distortions derive from differences in status and authority. The point is that there is ample room for error in examining others' speaking patterns, and one of those errors can be a circularity of judgment, counterjudgment, suspicion, and accusation of the sort that plagued Herod and his regime.[1] I will return to the question of how the observer's view may differ from that of the actors in the next chapter.

[1] Even in modern societies, linguistic competence is often an essential ingredient in recipes for social status; in traditional societies, where language is perhaps the fundamental social institution, oratory and rhetorical mastery are avenues to social mobility as well as necessary equipment for the defense of social status. On the role of rhetoric in Greco-Roman society, see Stambaugh and Balch 1986: 122.

It is also important to note that in the Hellenized cities of the empire Jews would have been exposed on a daily basis to the language and gestures of ethnic groups as foreign to them in certain respects as are the Chinese to American businessmen in the example given above in the text. As Stambaugh and Balch put it, "casual expressions of traditional polytheistic piety were unavoidable in the normal cultural world of the cities in the first and second centuries CE" (1986: 107ff., 130).

In this constant exposure to social dramas in which others engage in ritualized expressions of piety and devotion, often if not entirely for the sake of public display, it would be understandable for individuals to become not only skeptical but suspicious

What troubled Herod has troubled many rulers both before and since the first century: for example, how to know whether the deference of subordinates is real or feigned. Some forms of deference are no doubt given with both heart and mind; other shows of deference, such as those Herod suspected, were given only because the sons, servants, slaves, and soldiers feared for their lives. In a footnote on this subject, Runciman (1989: 88) notes that "deference may be accorded *hypocritically* – that is, willingly but without conviction," just as it may be given unwillingly. In either event, he reminds us, it is still "deference," and can be *described* as such. It is only when we take up the task of *interpreting* the sources of inspiration and the approaches to authority in which deference is shown or withheld that we must take into account whether the inspiration comes only from the mind, only from the heart or, in fact, from neither of the two.

It is in language that a society may be seen to be having more or less difficulty in reproducing itself. In this chapter I wish to illustrate this process of linguistic self-production in a variety of ways. In each case the relation of language to reality becomes increasingly problematical as individuals engage in various roles. Under these conditions, individuals become not merely persons, as it were, but role-performers. At that moment the gap between language and reality can widen. As it becomes wider, I will suggest, so does the gap between the authority and the inspiration with which the role itself is being performed. This gap only becomes intensely problematical, however, when the spiritual stakes for the community or nation are relatively high, but that need not prevent us from using examples drawn from less strenuous occasions.

Now, authority has many dimensions, and it will be necessary to make some distinctions. For instance, I will illustrate how individuals are discredited by being considered inauthentic. Josephus describes a number of ways that members of Herod's household were discredited: for example, by attention to a

of others' motives and intentions. The surface of social interaction would not inspire confidence, however smooth were the exchanges in the market-place. Attributions of hypocrisy and even of ill-will might become common projections of individuals' doubts about the authority and authenticity of their own ritual observances.

difference between their demeanor and their tone of voice. When the lack of authenticity becomes pervasive, speech becomes a way of masking intentions, exposing others' hypocrisy, and maintaining a distance between what is said in public and what is spoken in private. In reporting these conversations, Josephus mentions more than a lack of authenticity: he describes how authority works – and fails to work – when individuals do not know what they are talking about, that is, when they lack credibility in a world of secrets and spies. He also describes how traditional authority depends on public displays of approval and trust by the public on state occasions, so that the failure of such displays reflects a weakening of authority. Remember the 1960s slogan: "Suppose they gave a war and nobody came?" Herod had to worry that his public displays, in games, theaters, and spectacles, would not be greeted by the requisite shouts of approval from the Jewish masses. Simply to describe a crisis in the legitimation of authority in a system such as the Herodian kingdom, it is therefore necessary to report on ordinary conversations, confrontations, appeals, and other less dramatic linguistic encounters. There the pervasive aspect of the crisis becomes apparent in the widespread discrediting of each person who has a role in the drama. Suspicion and paranoia become institutionalized.

There is another reason for keeping our level of observation on ordinary language. Berger has called language the most basic of social institutions: more fundamental than the family or education, for instance, both of which are part of any society's foundations. If language is so fundamental a part of social order, it follows that, when speech is disturbed, an entire society can be disrupted. In this chapter I will seek to show what it was like to live in Herod's kingdom by citing a few brief but poignant comments that Josephus makes concerning the fear, melancholy, and hard-heartedness of the times. In moving, then, from description to interpretation, we will see why language is important: not despite the fact that it is problematical, but precisely because its relation to reality is problematical.

As I mentioned in chapter 2, to interpret social facts requires us to consider *what it was like* to live within a particular social context, but it also requires that we look for *corollaries*: for related events that are part of the larger pattern. A society in which authority is largely considered to be legitimate will reproduce itself in most, if not all, of its linguistic encounters. People who are entitled to respect will be addressed by their titles; appeals will be made with deference to those in authority. As in the case of the Chinese businessmen that I discussed at the beginning of this chapter, the shape of a discussion will reflect the speakers' concerns for maintaining the good-will and respect of others; that is why the Chinese preferred to build up slowly to their conclusions, whether they were making requests or demands. Legitimacy requires and permits each speaker to display concern for the attention, well-being, and consent of others; otherwise speech becomes an exchange of mutually incompatible demands or lapses into hostile silence. Indeed, Herod eventually refused to admit his sons Aristobulus and Alexander to his "conversation" and to his "table."

In interpreting the crisis in legitimacy in Herod's regime, I will therefore look for ways in which that illegitimate authority reproduced itself in each new encounter.[2] Herod turned to killing the bearers of bad news and executed the accusers along with the accused. Words turned to what Josephus called "poison." Those inspired with the spirit of truth were killed along with the deceivers. Conversely, Herod was significantly accused by one of his own military commanders of having lost his own legitimacy because his soul was "empty." I will return to that speech later in this chapter.[3]

SEPARATING LEVELS OF ANALYSIS FROM LEVELS OF OBSERVATION: THE BEGINNINGS OF EXPLANATION

How, finally, to *explain* the divorce of inspiration from authority? The answer to that question requires us to distinguish between

---

[2] This is the sociological way of inquiring into what Josephus called the same "evil genius" that inspired father and son, Herod and Antipater; as Cornfeld (1982: 118, nn. 628(a) and 632(a)) suggests, that satanic mind was the product of their interaction over several years, including the father's exiling the son.

[3] The control of fathers over sons in Roman society, which the Herodian household was no doubt copying, is the subject of some telling comments by Stambaugh and Balch 1986: 124.

the "level" of observation, which in our case is ordinary speech, and the "level" of analysis. In this chapter I will focus on roles: the cluster of actions that typify an individual who acts in his or her capacity as a member of a family or of a community.

Role, for some sociologists, is a term with meanings borrowed from the theater. A role enables a person to play a social part; his or her speech is therefore partly prescribed, partly a creation of the person. Some sociologists would focus on the ways that an individual creates a role or plays one; the audience is therefore an essential aspect of the role and its performance. Other sociologists, who view social life less as a drama than as a set of structures and processes, see the role as the elementary unit of social organization: the cell, as it were, in the tissues of the body politic. Thus individuals are likely to be seen as taking roles rather than as creating or playing them. Some sociologists have gone so far as to think of the social order in organic terms, so that the processes by which roles are filled and taken resemble the metabolism of the human body as it seeks to reproduce itself. In this introductory essay on method, I am borrowing a little from each perspective. By focusing on the problematic nature of role performances, I am enlarging on the view of social life as a drama, in which actors play out their roles with more or less authenticity, credibility, and authority before an audience that is more or less skeptical or enthralled.

In asking how the Herodian regime sought to renew itself through the succession of the sons to the father's role, I am exhibiting a typical sociological concern with how societies reproduce themselves. The point, however, is simply that our level of analysis is shifting away from the ways that various persons construe actions into acts; our analysis now moves upward to the ways individuals, as role-performers, go about speaking with various degrees of authority and inspiration, that is, to how they carry conviction in their roles. The move is "upward" in the sense that we are focusing somewhat higher on the ladder of social structure: not on actions as such but on actions-organized-by-roles-into-practices.

Nothing else has changed. Our focus (level of observation) is still on the way that individuals turn the chaos of social action into well-defined acts: through letters and conversations, accusations and appeals, testimony and lies, secrets and confessions, and through all the other speech-acts that are typical of trials whether in Caesar's court or in everyday life. Our focus also remains primarily on the members of Herod's family, entourage, and administration.[4] We are still looking at how these utterances carried conviction or failed to move the audience. Now, however, we shall be analyzing the roles themselves. What are they? To whom is each role played, as if before an audience? Who are the others engaged with the particular actor in his or her performance?

Our *level of analysis* has therefore shifted. We are asking how *roles* are filled: by chance, by choice, by inheritance, by merit, by election? How, then, did the Herodian regime seek to reproduce itself from one generation to the next? The level of analysis therefore concerns the system's way of reproducing itself and not merely the Herodian crisis of succession. We want to know how the crisis of succession under Herod affected Israel's ability to renew itself. While we cannot begin to answer these questions here, we can begin to sketch out a plan for answering them.

The "problematic" has not changed. We are still concerning ourselves with the tenuous connection between language and reality. We still want to know how actions are construed into acts through one kind of speaking or another. That is, we are concerned, as before, with how basic social facts are constructed: the entire lexicon of acts in a given society. Whether these are acts of compassion or Acts of Congress, they constitute the hard core, as it were, of social life. The problematic remains the same, that is, to examine the role of language in this process of social reconstruction. The way that language is used to construe actions into acts depends, first of all, on how speech is related to specific contexts and to actual deeds. In the second place, the role of language depends on how speech transcends those contexts and cuts across social categories and boundaries. That

---

[4] If this preoccupation with the distortions and secrecy in the palace seems somewhat extreme, consider Cornfeld's comment that Herod's "court was steeped in mutual hatred and suspicion and showed all the signs typical of an Oriental palace and harem in which the rule of its aging monarch is drawing to a close" (1982: 110, n. 563(d)). Such chronic sedition was no doubt enhanced because the status of women was hardly different from "chattels," as Cornfeld puts it.

is why we keep our focus on what people say and how they say it: to whom, with what emphasis and intonation, where, and with what impact or consequences.

Now, however, we are analyzing this process at the "level" of role-performances. Actors are now going to be analyzed as they are being recruited or tested before being allowed to take on certain roles. They will be seen speaking their lines with varying degrees of authority and inspiration and carrying more or less conviction with their fellow performers and their audiences. In this process, moreover, a society is finding new recruits to take on roles as older performers retire, die, or are dispensed with for one reason or another.

A society can thus be analyzed in the process of reproducing itself. In fact, new roles may be generated that were not there before. The birth of new forms, that is, new roles, is of particular significance for the relationship of language to reality. They may fill the gap between what is said and what is actually done; they may help language to transcend certain contexts or barriers. Indeed, I would argue that the Jesus movement may have played a significant role precisely in this birth of new roles and networks through forms of speech that left little doubt as to what was said or done as well as through inspired forms of utterance that crossed hitherto impassable barriers.[5] More on that subject when we turn to the development of new religious groups and movements. The point is that, without changing our level of observation, we may raise our level of analysis.

After suggesting how to describe the widening gap between language and reality as individuals perform their roles, the task still remains of interpreting what it is like to live in a system where authority itself is involved in a crisis of legitimacy. *When the entire system suffers from a lack of credibility, the crisis at the top, so to speak, reproduces itself in ordinary conversation and everyday encounters.* We are no longer inquiring merely into a crisis of succession

---

[5] Consider this passage, for instance, as a starting point for inquiry: "But beware of men, for they will deliver you up to the councils, and they will scourge you in their synagogues; and ye shall be brought before governors and kings for my sake, for a testimony against them and the Gentiles. But when they deliver you up, take no thought how or what you shall speak: for it shall be given you in that same hour what ye shall speak" (Matthew 10: 17–19).

within a regime, but asking what it is like to endure a crisis in the way a society reproduces itself in the speech-acts of everyday life. Finally, however, our task is to *explain* the widening gap between language and reality at the level of roles and their performances.

NETWORKS: ANOTHER LEVEL OF ANALYSIS

Just a word on that subject at this point may help to introduce a key term: the *network* of roles in any society. The gap between language and reality (and at the level of roles, the gap between authority and inspiration) is partially due to the separation of role-networks. A "network" lies somewhere between a group and a coalition: far less organized than a group, but with a more continuous and "dense" social life than coalitions, which may exist for specific purposes and the time being without having a life of their own. A network of roles circumscribes what is said, to whom, in what manner, and with what shared assumptions and understandings. The network consists of persons who – as performers of certain roles – take each other into account. They are like what used to be called in earlier essays on the sociology of roles a "reference group": a set of people in roles who take each other into account as they go about their performances, whether or not they actually meet to discuss their affairs. A network, I would add, *does* involve communication: more or less frequent, more or less understandable by outsiders, and more or less open to outside influence. Some networks are closed; outsiders, even when allowed to be present, often catch only the words but not the music: that is, only the obvious meaning of what is said, and not its real, underlying meaning. That implicit meaning is known only to those who have "ears to hear." In any event, I will be suggesting that, given the "problematic" that we have chosen, namely the complex and ambiguous relation of language to reality, it would be helpful to examine the networks of role performers to see who is communicating with whom along various channels.

In Herod's family and administration, I will suggest, we may find an example of networks which are also to be found in the larger society at the same time. Herod's immediate social world, then, might be a microcosm within which we can see close-up what was also going on in Israel and in that part of the Roman empire at the time. For instance, men were being frustrated and yet also at times aided by women in the pursuit of authority and its exercise; slaves and eunuchs were being employed, bribed, and subverted by those with some interest of their own to pursue or maintain; the military and the priesthood appear on stage occasionally in roles that either conflict with Herod or support his designs; Jews and Romans, Arabs and Syrians, also have roles to play in this drama and threaten Herod's ability to reproduce his rule from one generation to the next. It is fathers and sons, however, who seem to have the central parts in this drama; and, I will suggest, it is the network of sons that seems to have in common the most clear-cut interests in the succession to royal power: interests that are thwarted, however, when their lineage stems from mothers of different ethnic backgrounds or hereditary status (or when one, like Antipater, was born to Herod when Herod was a private rather than a public man). Of course, it is not at all unusual for a corporation like the nobility to be divided internally in ways that mimic the larger society. Runciman (1989: 108) notes that in eighteenth-century France the nobility (as well as the clergy and the third estate) were divided within themselves along lines that could be found outside the nobility. The division between fathers and sons, I am suggesting, is one crucial line of division in first-century Palestine.[6]

In this preliminary excursion into the area, however, I am simply trying to develop a method for asking the right questions, that is, for defining a problematic. As Runciman (1989: 88) reminds us, moreover, "there is no need to dismiss out of hand the literary evidence of contemporary observers." If Josephus is

---

[6] In the following passage from Matthew, for instance, is a description of the "day of judgment", but it may have had a more than eschatological resonance in the ears of a community that had been penetrated by Herodian spies and informers and in families that were divided both within and between generations along lines that were also political: "And the brother shall deliver up the brother to death, and the father the child: and the children shall rise up against *their* parents, and cause them to be put to death" (Matthew 10: 21). Very similar observations can be made of contemporary Iraq under the Ba'athist party; cf. Samir al-Khalil 1989.

at all accurate, then, somewhere near the bottom of Herod's household we will find slaves and domestics, above which will be the women: the sisters and the mothers who are forming a network (Josephus calls it the "circle" of women) of their own. Into these networks, seeking information, infiltrate informers like Herod's sister, Salome, and outsiders: guests of the palace who make the most of their opportunities to find out what is going on and to exercise influence. Above them come the generations of sons and brothers: Herod and his brother Pheroras; Antipater and his half-brothers Alexander and Aristobulus. In the wings of each stratum of brothers lie Herod's sons by his many other wives: each a potential claimant to the line of succession. The household occasionally entertains priests and officers in the military who come bringing news, much of it bad. Given Herod's monopoly of power not only over his family but over the military and the market-place, and given his attempt at control of the priesthood and his patronage of the Temple which he constructed, it is therefore necessary to consider these other orders of the state and church as part of his regime. Finally, of course, his regime involves important relationships to other rulers. We shall therefore consider how Herod's authority, like much of his inspiration, depended on his relation with Caesar Augustus himself, who eventually demotes Herod from the status of "friend" to that of mere "subject." In all these cases we find examples of roles which are more or less authoritative, as Runciman puts it,

whether in relation to seniority, leadership, wealth, actual or fictive pedigree, prestige ritual, access to means of coercion, or rights over land or property of other kinds. (1989: 91)

In the light of Runciman's discussion of how roles differ in authority, we would not be surprised to find that sons, even in Herod's family, could not all be considered equal in these respects. They differed markedly from each other in what I would call access to the means of production of legitimate authority. The pedigree of some was better than that of others; Glaphyra, the wife of Alexander and daughter of King Archelaus of Antioch, was apparently not amused that the wife of Aristobulus should consider herself an equal. The status of sons could be marked, then, by the marriages arranged for them and not only by their pedigree. Certainly they differed in pedigree, seniority, access to "prestige ritual," in leadership, and in their rights to land and wealth: Herod saw to that. (That is why I do not want to use Runciman's term, systact, to refer to occupants of roles who form a network with enduring, substantive interests: see Runciman 1989: 20ff.) None the less, it may well be that sons often formed networks of their own, either within a context such as the Herodian regime or in specific religious movements that emphasized brotherly love and recruited their members from sons unsure of their opportunities or rights of succession to their fathers.

Here I wish to suggest only that the relation of what was said to what was done depended on networks, and that these networks were not only solutions to the problem of trusting what others said but were also part of the problem itself. They put new barriers between language and certain kinds of reality. Thus, what was said within a network might have a specific meaning relevant only to that context. Certainly those young men evading the draft in the Vietnam War must have had their codes and hidden meanings as well as lines of communication. So did the brothers united in religious groups or guerilla movements in first-century Palestine. The very existence of these networks, however, put up barriers to communication that could be crossed only by the most trusted teachers and leaders.

DESCRIPTION

Josephus occasionally gives chilling descriptions of the skill and deception employed by key actors in Herod's family in the performance of their roles. It would therefore be well to remember the context in which such performances were enacted. Josephus points out that

among his [Herod's] own people if anyone was not deferential to him in speech by confessing himself his slave or was thought to be raising questions about his rule, Herod was unable to control himself and prosecuted his kin and his friends alike, and punished them as severely as his enemies. (*Antiquities* XVI.5.4; Josephus 1969: 269)

There is no mention of a court jester whose job it was to speak unpalatable truths and so to close the gap between language and reality. Herod enjoyed a near monopoly on power; when it came to occupying his role as king, only Caesar could unseat him. As for controlling the succession, he had a virtual right to choose his successors from among his sons, although they could not claim the title or be sure of their appointment without Caesar's approval. Succession, then, was clearly the only prize worth having, since it was the key to economic, military, and symbolic sources of power, but the ultimate basis for legitimacy of succession lay outside Herod's control.

Under these conditions, it is understandable that anyone in line for the succession should take careful precautions to manage the impressions he might be giving. Antipater, whose plots to eliminate his rivals, the brothers Alexander and Aristobulus, caused havoc in the Herodian succession, accused his brothers privately, but in public came to their defense "that this show of goodwill might make him seem trustworthy in the hostile moves which he was planning" (*Antiquities* xvi.7.2; Josephus 1969: 285).[7]

More is clearly involved here than the skilled manipulation of appearances, although certainly such performances were necessary for survival, even if they were not sufficient to ensure a place in the succession of sons to their father's authority. Indeed, more is involved than the split between what is said in public and what is spoken only privately, although this split, like the split between appearance and reality in role performances, can undermine public speech to the point that no authority can be considered trustworthy. *Under these conditions, no society can reproduce itself.*

Certainly Antipater "was somehow very clever in making his

---

[7] The careful manipulation of public appearances when the succession to authority is at stake is noticed by Tacitus as well; speaking of the days following the succession of Tiberius to the throne left empty by Augustus, he writes: "Meanwhile at Rome consuls, senate, knights, precipitately became servile. The more distinguished men were, the greater their urgency and insincerity. They must show neither satisfaction at the death of one emperor, nor gloom at the accession of another: so their features were carefully arranged in a blend of tears and smiles, mourning and flattery" (1956;1988: 35).

associates believe in the friendship that he feigned, and was also very adroit in concealing the hatred that he felt for everyone" (*Antiquities* xvii.1.1; Josephus 1969: 377). To a few, of course, he confided his real feelings about his rivals. Although Josephus is not entirely specific about who was in Antipater's network, we may infer that it included several women: notably Antipater's mother, the wife of Herod's brother Pheroras, and that wife's mother and sister. This is the "circle" of women that controlled Pheroras and set him at odds with Alexander and Aristobulus. Like Antipater, these women were skilled performers:

And finding that their friendship was hateful to the king, they schemed to keep their meetings from being known and to make a show of hating and reviling each other whenever there was an opportunity, especially when Herod was present or any who were likely to report to him, but secretly they made their friendly understanding even stronger. (*Antiquities* xvii.2.4)[8]

As I will point out later, under the rubric of "explanation," there is a circular pattern here. Starting with monopolistic authority in search of legitimacy, competition with rivals for succession to authority, inauthentic role performances, and the development of closed networks, the process feeds on itself as the closed networks develop their own sources of inspiration, limit their communications with outsiders, and keep their social distance from those in authoritative roles. It is enough to make any authority unsure of itself. To be sure of itself, authority must be legitimate: that is, it must be seen to be inspired by the same sources that inspire the people themselves. The growth of closed networks, whether in the household of Herod or in the Galilean countryside, cuts at the ties linking public authority with private devotion.

It is not surprising, then, that Herod put on shows himself: not the petty shows of conviviality that graced the inauthentic performances of members of his household, but grand shows indeed. Herod financed games, spectacles, combats; he procured for them the best fighters and athletes, musicians and

---

[8] Of course, these were not the first women to oppose Herod. For an extended discussion of Hasmonean women, one of whom in particular held a fortress against Herod after the death of her brother Antigonus, see Sievers 1989: 141.

dancers that his money, exacted from both Jew and gentile, could buy. The purpose of these shows, Josephus reminds us, was to dramatize the largeness of Herod's spirit. The stadium, the theater, and the temple were the arenas in which he "publicly made his generosity famous" (*Antiquities* XVI.5.1; Josephus 1969: 263). Like all performances, however, these public displays required acclamation and applause; otherwise they would have failed in their function of joining popular with official sources of inspiration. Some Jews, however, boycotted these spectacles because they were distasteful to their religion; as Josephus pointed out, these Jews were unable therefore "to flatter the king's ambition with statues or temples," just as they could not join in the public acclaim of his generosity in these public displays (*Antiquities* XVI.5.4; Josephus 1969: 271). Granting Josephus' desire to provide an apologetic for the Jews' refusal of acclaim for Herodian rule, still, as a native informer, Josephus has a point. The circle of display must be widened to include public acclaim so that Herod's authority can claim legitimacy. The king can refuse his subjects an audience; the subjects, however, can refuse to be an audience for the king. Traditional loyalties and beliefs, dramatized in displays and rites, or authority of a more personal kind that depends on the authenticity of the performer (whether Antipater, the circle of women, or Herod displaying the "generosity of his soul") were respectively the hard and soft currency of social credit.

Such credit, according to Josephus, was in short supply; certainly Herod had trouble knowing who were falsely accusing his sons Aristobulus and Alexander and who were telling the truth. It was then quite literally the case that "a man's foes *be* those of his own household" (Matthew 10:39). Herod's own credibility in accusing his sons depended on the credibility of his sources. Josephus therefore records numerous cases of torture, by which Herod tried to extract the truth, but the fact of torture made the confessions and revelations of conspiracy even more questionable.[9]

[9] It is perhaps in this context that one might look again at sayings of Jesus that clearly refer to torture and imprisonment: perhaps they contain not only eschatological references but veiled allusions to facts of Palestinian life under the Herodians or direct

Herod himself was accused before Caesar in Rome of having invaded Arabia and having killed 2,500 soldiers defending a garrison (*Antiquities* xvi.9, 10). The accuser was Sylleus, an Arab who had insinuated his way into Herod's favor and tried – but failed – to marry Salome, Herod's sister. His revenge was to lie to Caesar; Sylleus concealed an unpaid debt of his to Herod, neglected to mention that Herod had permission from the president of Syria to recover that debt by force, and exaggerated the Arabs' military losses enormously. The campaign of "disinformation" worked, and Herod found himself, as I have mentioned, demoted by Caesar from friend to mere subject (*Antiquities* xvi.9.3). The damage done to Herod's credibility (and hence authority) was severe, but Josephus goes on to point out that Herod was overcome by "fear and despair":

All this was Herod forced to endure, since the freedom of action which had been given him by Caesar was gone, and he lost a good deal of his spirit. (*Antiquities* xvi.9.4; Josephus 1969: 327)

It would be hard to find a clearer expression of the intimate relation of inspiration to legitimate authority. The Caesar who is "lord and savior" of all can withhold favor and so darken the spirit of even the most powerful king of the Jews. Herod himself became depressed and anxious, as though the spirit of authority had left him exposed as an emperor, so to speak, without clothes.[10]

INTERPRETATION

The depressed spirit of Herod is one clue to what it was like to live in a society where the sources of inspiration had parted company with those in authority. The crisis in legitimacy proliferated, as Herod "was thoroughly outraged and filled with fears . . . His mistrust and hatred were directed against all"

Roman rule. Cf. "And fear not them which kill the body, but are not able to kill the soul: but rather fear him which is able to destroy both soul and body in hell" (Matthew 10: 28).

[10] For a brief discussion of the title of "friend" of Caesar, see Schürer–Vermes–Millar (1973: 316). It is clear that the title conferred a "special distinction," although it was neither hereditary nor in all cases public.

(*Antiquities* XVI.8.2; Josephus 1969: 303). All were suspect: if Herod should fall out of favor, then all should fall out of favor with Herod. In other words the system kept acting like a system, one central part of which (Herod's regime) affected the whole. The consistent pattern of discrediting produced a systemic crisis of legitimacy that made any role virtually untenable.[11]

A close analogy might be the era of Stalin, in which Stalin used informers, spies, secret police, torture, and assassination to arrive at information while the truth kept eluding him. No one was safe, since no one had the right to incumbency in any role within the regime if they fell from Stalin's favor. An even closer analogy may be Iraq under Hussein and the Ba'athist party, which is self-consciously modeled on Stalinism and totalitarian one-party rule. Indeed, no aspect of Iraqi society, including the intimate lives of families, is immune to the penetration of the party, and children do in fact, wittingly or unwittingly, cause their parents' disappearance into party cells and dungeons, from which many simply do not return.[12] A personal administration, one that rules through the dispensing of favor, thus turns into quasi-universal disfavor; no one is exempt from the terror of being discredited. Josephus notes that Herod was occasionally repentant of the harm he inflicted on those he found disloyal but continued to make everyone suffer, including the accusers themselves (*Antiquities* XVI.8.2). Torture itself failed, since it produced either more lies or mere silence (*Antiquities* XVI.8.4).

The breakdown in legitimacy was therefore apparent to everyone in the administration, including a military officer named Tiro, who exercised what Josephus called "the greatest boldness" in telling Herod the truth. Usually an officer speaks with authority when he or she stays within the limits of the

[11] Schürer–Vermes–Millar note that Herod "set out to smother in embryo every attempt at insurrection by means of rigorous police measures. Loitering in the streets, gatherings, indeed even walking together, was forbidden. And where anything contrary was done, the king heard of it immediately through his spies. He is even said sometimes to have acted the spy himself" (1973: 315). Of course, these attempts to turn the country into a nation of informers would increase the gap between speech and reality, as all communication became guarded and inauthentic.

[12] Samir al-Khalil writes, "The fact is Ba'athism modeled itself self-consciously, as a movement and in power, on Stalinist norms" (1989: 97–98).

official role. In a crisis, however, speech cannot be so easily contained within its customary context; in this case, another function of language, that is, to transcend social contexts, was not being fulfilled. The officer in question, Tiro, therefore said that he "preferred this bold outspokenness to my own safety" in order to transcend the customary and official limits that ordinarily give an official's words force and authority (*Antiquities* XVI.9.5; Josephus 1969: 361).

To close the gap between language and reality thus requires innovation in roles: new ways of taking old roles or, if that should fail, new roles in which one can speak the previously unspeakable truth. Tiro approached Herod with the truth that he had lost his sources of inspiration; it is as if not only his mind had strayed but his inner being were lost or empty (*Antiquities* XVI.11.5). The secret of Herod's despair was therefore not a secret at all: Tiro tells Herod that his soldiers are in favor of his sons, Alexander and Aristobulus, and against Herod himself; their right to the succession, then, was being confirmed by the military even when it was being denied by Herod himself. Note, then, Herod's loss of control over the military, as evidenced by Tiro's freedom to speak directly to Herod without permission or signs of deference, and by the soldiers' reported defection to the side of his sons. Note also Herod's loss of legitimacy (as well as his loss of control over the means of sheer force and coercion). The loss of legitimacy clearly derives from the emptiness of Herod's soul, as it were: the loss of his own inspiration. It sets the stage for religious movements by "kings" who are quite sure of their own legitimacy and inspiration.

The crisis of legitimation thus spreads, as the system expresses itself in these encounters. Even in this exchange, where innovation occurs, Herod reproduces the cycle of fear and discredit by jailing Tiro as well as the officers whom Tiro names as being loyal to Herod's sons. After due process has been observed by calling an assembly, all the officers are stoned to death. The gap between language and reality widens until the sources of truth-telling themselves have been silenced.

The reality of a regime founded on lies and suspicion is then made impermeable to internal change, and the circles of suspicion widen to include eventually the source of the lies, Antipater himself. His trial will occupy us in the next chapter. Here I simply want to note that *the systemic effects of a crisis in legitimacy can make it impossible for a society to reproduce itself*. It is a simple interpretation of the corollaries of Herod's crisis of succession, but it has implications for the sociology of religion.

RETURNING TO THE TASK OF INTERPRETATION: MELANCHOLY AND DREAD

What, then, was it like to live in a society that was threatened with systemic self-destruction and with a tissue of lies so thick as to blanket the truth permanently? As a native informant, Josephus tells us that *"silence and sadness darkened the former splendor of the palace"* (*Antiquities* xvi.8.5; Josephus 1969: 313; my italics). This is a particularly interesting statement, since it goes far beyond the usual hearsay and tradition, oral or written, on which Josephus has been relying for this reconstruction of the crisis of succession. A feeling is being attributed to the kingdom: a loss of its inner well-being or "eudaimonism." On the face of it, it is not absurd. Anyone who has lived through the days immediately following the assassination of Martin Luther King and John F. Kennedy will understand that a nation can be deeply affected by the fate of its leaders. The feeling here of melancholy, however, could be due to several sources, and it may be useful simply to note the methodological questions raised by its use.

Studies of melancholy usually introduce some distinctions in the general feeling. Freud himself distinguished melancholia from grief: melancholia being the inner feeling of identification with someone who has died. The death of the person may be real or imagined, and in the case of sons who have wished to kill their fathers, the death of the father may be purely imaginary, but no less real in its psychological consequences. Melancholia may then be like a fear of being pursued by a "dead" father, or it may come from the son's identification with the father who has been killed – in imagination – by the son. Melanie Klein distinguishes the anxiety that stems from an actual loss (i.e. a melancholy depression that expresses the feeling of loss or of being lost without someone) from another emotion, which she terms persecutory anxiety. The latter anticipates the retaliation of someone who has been killed, if only in the imagination, and who may therefore be either dead or alive. The two feelings are not exclusive of each other, and an individual may harbor them at the same time. Consider, then, what a people might be feeling who have been clearly on the side of Herod's sons and have come to hate Herod himself. They may desire the father to be killed and so dread his vengeance; on the other hand, they may be anticipating the death of his sons: a death over which they despair but which they cannot prevent. Melancholy is not too strong a word for such a pervasive feeling of combined dread and despair.

Interpretation of this sort clearly goes beyond the limits of sociology and enters the realm of psychoanalytic discourse. I draw on Freud and Klein precisely in order to suggest that sociological method, left to its own devices, can be remarkably indifferent to what people experience in some depth. There is a psychoanalytic tradition within sociology, however, which does seek to understand the very powerful links between persons and their roles. Even the role of the ordinary citizen or subject, who closely identifies with the leadership of the nation, can be a very serious role indeed for precisely the reasons that Freud and Klein have given. When a people lose their head of state (for instance, through assassination, war, or execution), they are likely to lose their own heads, that is, to panic. Melancholy solitude may be a defense against panic: a way of stemming a very profound fear of loss and chaos. Because Herod, after all, had lost his own confidence, his soldiers had lost confidence in him, and panic may not have been far from their innermost feelings at such a time.

Interpretations can only offer various ways of looking at social life: they are particularly important schemata when one is trying to grasp what it was like to live at a certain time. The interpretations suggested by Klein and Freud, who sense panic or at least profound anxiety in the minds of individuals, do help to make sense of some further observations by Josephus himself.

The following passage refers not only to grief and sorrow but to something closer to panic itself. The context is a gathering at Caesarea: a new gathering to put Alexander and Aristobulus on trial:

When he came to Caesarea, everyone at once began to talk about his sons, and the kingdom was in suspense as people waited to see what would be done with them. *For a terrible fear seized them all* that the long dispute between the two sides would now reach its (tragic) end . . . It was not possible, however, either to say anything impulsive or to hear another say it without danger, but *they kept their pity locked within them,* and so they bore their excessive suffering with pain but *at the same time without speaking.* (*Antiquities* XVI.9.4; Josephus 1969: 359, my italics)

Note the resonances with the passages in the New Testament, some of them apocalyptic, in which the people are in "great expectation" and men's hearts are failing them because of fear. These passages may also resonate because they share a common rhetorical source with Josephus in public discourse or classical literature. Note also, moreover, that Josephus is stressing the departure of language from social reality; and suffering that was "excessive" was all the more unbearable because one could not speak safely and freely. In the absence of a publicly acknowledged truth, suffering is compounded.

Certainly the dramatization of a sacrifice of a son destined to rule is mirrored in the gospel narratives and may suggest that, on the periphery of the kingdom, the sacrifice of Herod's sons to his jealous rage may have been felt very keenly for a long time throughout the society.[13] The resonance of the gospel narratives with these events may at least carry a reminiscence of the earlier tragedy. On the other hand, the fate of sons at the hands of their fathers was clearly a more general condition, a more common

---

[13] Of course, I mean to suggest a range of crises from the Herodian to the average household. Is it possible, for instance, that the following saying embodies a recollection of what was said of Herod during his lifetime? "If they called the master of the house Be-elzebub, how much more shall they call them of his household" (Matthew 10: 25). In the Gospel of Matthew, furthermore, there are many other sayings about the divisions within ordinary households between generations, between in-laws, and between brothers and sisters. It is as if every household were a reflection of the Herodian household, as well as a victim of Herodian repression.

fate, that goes far beyond the tragedy of Herod's sons or the fate of religious prophets like Jesus.[14]

In assessing motives and feelings we are probing the borders between interpretation and explanation. Repressed hatred of sons toward fathers and of citizens toward their leaders may underlie much of the distortions, deception, and emptiness of speech. Now, however, attention must shift to explanation, where we must look for obvious structural causes rather than psychological interpretations of the melancholic stalemate we have been discussing.

EXPLANATION

How is it that communication between a father and his sons can become so distorted that the father can believe in every accusation and even come to hate his sons personally? Josephus notes that Herod had previously hated them in his role as king, but eventually came to hate them *himself* (*Antiquities* XVI.10.2): a statement that suggests the extent to which the paranoia inspired by the role was intensified (and perhaps fed) by his own paranoid fears. Certainly it would be a mistake to ignore the personal sources of Herod's paranoia, but how do we explain the breakdown of his confidence in his role, especially in relation to his own sons Alexander and Aristobulus, who had the most to lose from any suspicion of betrayal on their part and who had been in line for the succession? After the initial trial before Caesar, when the appearance of reconciliation displaced Herod's misgivings, what could account for the circular process of suspicion, fear, and accusation?

---

[14] Cornfeld notes that Herod himself appealed to "the ancient customs empowering a father to condemn his rebellious son (Deut. 21, 18–22)" (1982: 108, n. 540(a)). It is difficult to imagine a more acute dilemma than that faced by a people who wished simultaneously to rebel and yet to maintain the ancient authority of the patriarch over sons. It is likely, I would suggest, that a number of religious movements, including the Jesus movement, were expressions – and attempted resolutions – of that dilemma. This extremely painful "double-bind" is known to produce forms of mental disturbance and of innovations in speech.

The network of roles in which the sons shared their fears and hopes was separate from their father's network, in one respect at least, even from the outset: they were subordinate in a system that gave fathers a power over their sons that a modern parent would find extraordinary and unconscionable. The sheer fact of inequality does impede communication; subordinates are not on equal terms with their superiors and are obliged, as we have seen in the case of members of Herod's household, to maintain their positions by continual displays of deference.

Consider, by way of a very modest contemporary analogy, the behavior of English-speaking South Asians in a British factory, whose gestures of deference were intended to avoid conflict with their supervisors but, in some cases, heightened their supervisor's suspicions. Jupp et al. (1982: 232–256) report that one supervisor, who had been quite suspicious of a South Asian woman assigned to her unit, greeted the news of that woman's assignment with the remark, "they've really pulled the wool over my eyes": "they" being the management responsible for placing the Asian woman in that supervisor's unit. The supervisor complained of the operative that "she'd never look at me," while other operatives of the same ethnic background explained that this sort of avoidance was necessary in order not to arouse the suspicion and anger of the supervisor, who was seen as excitable and arbitrary (Jupp et al. 1982: 240–241). The result is analogous with the circularity and escalation of communications in Herod's household: "Everyday problems and difficulties rapidly escalate into situations of stress and disciplinary procedures are invoked" (Jupp et al. 1982: 241).

Any network that is subordinate to those in authority and is separated by other characteristics, such as ethnicity or age, is likely to become relatively closed: that is, to keep its own secrets. Certainly Herod found it necessary to use spies and informers, along with various forms of inducement and coercion, to get what passed for information about his son's plans. Much of that information was disinformation planted by Antipater; much of it was distorted and fabricated under the pressures of fear and the pains of torture. Of course, the analogy with the South Asian operatives becomes stretched at this point, since the operatives' worst fear was simply losing their jobs, although such a loss could no doubt threaten the well-being of their families. Even under these comparatively benign conditions, however, the operatives tended to keep their own counsel. Jupp et al. report that they reacted negatively to the supervisor's attempts to get information: not an unusual reaction by those with relatively "low social power" (Jupp et al. 1982: 243). Their attempts to reduce their uncertainties and to secure their rights were then perceived as further evidence of a sullen, uncooperative, and perhaps disloyal spirit. The gap between public authority and private inspiration widens when the network of subordinates, already separated from those in authority by the facts of inequality in power and status, becomes closed to official inquiry.

Under these conditions, language – speech itself – becomes suspect, and those in authority tend to rely on non-verbal cues to form their impressions of subordinates' intentions. I have already noted the English supervisor's critical assessment of the demeanor of subordinates who would not look her in the face. On another occasion, Herod instructed Pheroras (his own brother) to scrutinize Salome and Sylleus, the Arab who later subverted Herod's position with Caesar. The two (Salome and Sylleus) were thought to be having an affair, and such a liaison might in fact have made Herod vulnerable to Arabian interests. Salome, furthermore, was a skilled dramatist. On another occasion, when accused of spreading a lie about Herod, she had torn her hair and beaten her breast, but, Josephus notes, "the malignity of her character proclaimed the insincerity of her actions" (*Antiquities* xvi.7.5; Josephus 1969: 295): signals that were harder to control than the more dramatic gestures of breast-beating and tearing the hair. Clearly the widespread contemporary interest in body language is neither new nor particularly modern, but characteristic of any social system marked by separate, unequal, and partially closed communication networks. None the less, symbolic gestures (body language) will have far more significance for an entire social system under the conditions obtaining in Palestine at the onset of the "Christian Era."[15]

The separate development of more or less closed networks provides an unusual opportunity for role-players who are especially adept at insinuating themselves into a set of relationships. As in the case of the sociologist, whose methods include what is called "participant observation" rather than spying, the object is none the less to gain inside information. The skills required are similar to those in spying: learning to read signals, to decipher what is said on the basis of what one knows about the personal background, social position, and values of each participant, and learning to understand what is at best only implied by words and gestures (cf. Gumperz 1982: 27). Under these conditions the sociologist, like a member of Herod's household, must become an expert in what is sometimes called "code-switching" and the use of "marked forms" (Gumperz 1982: 27). Codes may be dialects, but they may also be something less pronounced, for example, the use of tone of voice, emphasis, gesture, or key words to suggest where the speaker stands on a particular issue, regardless of what is stated for public consumption. These skills and practices help "in everyday situations [to] define the underlying assumptions with respect to which participants infer what is intended" (Gumperz 1982: 27). Only an adept could move into such a situation and gain the confidence of speakers sufficiently to get at information that could prove dangerous or even fatal.

Take, for example, the Lacedemonian Eurycles: an adept at spying if ever there was one. According to Josephus, Eurycles "gave him [Herod] presents and received even greater ones from him, and by the adroitness of his approach managed to become one of the closest friends of the kind" (*Antiquities* XVI.10.1; Josephus 1969: 331). To make a long story short,

---

[15] I do not mean to suggest that ancient Palestine was alone in this respect. Paul Veyne argues that Roman society itself, inegalitarian and status-conscious to an extreme, placed a very high premium on the proper exchange of gestures of greeting and deference. "Commoners were expected to address their betters with humility. Every gesture contributed to what Ramsey MacMullen has called 'the explicit expression of status'" (1987: 163).

Eurycles also befriended Herod's son Alexander, and by exaggerating whatever Alexander may have told him, gave Antipater further ammunition for his campaign against Alexander and Aristobulus.[16] After making this contribution to Alexander's eventual execution, Eurycles went to King Archelaus, Alexander's father-in-law, to report how he had succeeded in reconciling Herod to his son Alexander, for which "service" he was well paid with gifts from the grateful Archelaus.[17] Closed networks repay the closest ethnographic investigation, and they require the skills of a role-player of considerable virtuosity. However, the more individuals there are who are performing such roles tongue-in-cheek at considerable expense to their fellow players and to their audience, the more social life becomes a war of all against all: an arena in which only the most skilled performers survive. Under these conditions there may develop a strong but latent demand for deeds which do not need to be interpreted by words because "they speak for themselves": that is, in theological terms, for the "word" to be incarnated.

In this chapter I have been illustrating what can be gained by the careful choice of levels of observation and of analysis. Our "level of observation" has been speech in everyday life. There we have been looking at people engaging in closed or deceptive communication. We have also seen examples of individuals breaking out of their roles in order to speak the truth across various social barriers, like those separating the military from

[16] In a longer account in *The Jewish War*, Eurycles is said to have made his accusations to Herod himself, who was driven into "paroxysms of his persecution complex and ... a mortal hatred of his sons" (Cornfeld 1982: 106, n. 521(b)). In this and the succeeding note, Cornfeld observes that even Nicolaus, the author of the underlying account, may well have thought the two sons potentially capable of parricide. The record remains unclear, except with regard to the intensification of inter-generational fear, suspicion, and hatred.

[17] It may be that Eurycles was a typical figure of the adept who uses language to maintain a social position at the expense of others while nevertheless winning their gratitude. It may also be that to deplore such characters and their use of language fits a classical literary genre: cf. an instance in Tacitus' *The Annals of Imperial Rome* (1956;1988: 94), in which Tacitus observes that "This speech had a popular ring. But its effect was to safeguard Tiberius' dominant position."

other aspects of the regime or an officer from the head of state. Speech therefore becomes encapsulated in separate contexts (closed networks) or seeks to transcend these contexts in desperate attempts to say what must be said if a regime is to save itself. Our levels of analysis have been the role and role-network not merely within a regime but as an element of an entire system. The crisis of succession in Herod's regime is therefore a crisis in the legitimacy of all authority; in that crisis no one's authority, authenticity, or credibility can be taken for granted. Under these conditions a society may not be able to recruit sons to take their father's roles or be able to ensure that any roles will be filled by individuals who are prepared for them and committed to fulfilling them. A society under these conditions may not be able to reproduce itself. Herod's crisis, then, threatened the system as a whole with self-destruction. As we shall see in the next chapter, it also produced dramatic efforts by some to purify and renew the society's most important symbols and institutions.

There are some risks entailed in making the assumption that underlies the choice I have made in this chapter: to analyze what goes on in the face-to-face world of role-players in terms of an entire social system's struggle to reproduce itself. At the very least, I am assuming that the way individuals interact is part of the larger society's basic structure: not a question of fads and fashions, idiosyncrasies or mannerisms but closer to the type of civility which marks one as a member of the *civis*. A closer analogy would be to the symbolic behavior of the devotee, whose gestures of respect and penitence recreate a sacred order and allow that order to reproduce itself in the hearts and bodies of its followers. Under these conditions, crises at the head of a society resonate in the hearts of an entire people; panic can indeed set in, preceded by dread or melancholy. In less tightly integrated systems, of course, a lack of devotion and even widespread incivility may not be disruptive or threatening to a society, although even in a complex society such as the United States there may still be pressures to render the treatment of the flag a national political issue; some would even declare that such symbolic gestures as the treatment of the flag required constitutional sanctions. The point is that in a less coherent society such as the United States, conflict may be intense but less threatening to the ability of the social system to reproduce itself.

In a patriarchal society, however, the system depends on sons to fill the role of the father if the society is to recreate itself from one generation to the next; it correspondingly depends on women to recruit their daughters to fill roles of subordination to men. Controversy over the rights of children and the roles of women will therefore be of extreme importance to the survival of the society as a whole: not easily reduced to options, debates over child-rearing and life-styles, or even to various imputed rights to choice and self-determination. I will explore such controversies in Herod's regime further in the next chapter. Here I simply wish to observe that the rights of fathers over sons and the aspirations of sons to succeed their fathers were constitutive of Palestinian society as a whole. A lack of appropriate deference on the part of sons, like the loss of patriarchal authority by fathers, could shake the foundations of the entire system. When those conflicts make the relation of language to reality problematical, pressures mount for words that are as good as deeds; pressures also mount for authoritative speech that can transcend the barriers of particular contexts and overcome the limits imposed by subordinate social status. The implications for the study of prophetic and miraculous religious groups and movements, however, require separate treatment in terms of theories that would spell out these implications in clear but mutually exclusive terms. That task, of course, requires the discussion of theory at sufficient length for an entirely separate work from this brief essay on methodology.

CHAPTER 4

"What is going on here?"
The role of the observer and the beginnings of theory

TRIAL, SACRIFICE, OR COLLECTIVE SCAPEGOATING?
THE NEED FOR A THEORY

Even if there were no reason to question Josephus' version of events which he could not possibly have witnessed himself, the events themselves are ambiguous enough. Take the trials of the sons Alexander and Aristobulus for their alleged sedition against Herod. In the second chapter I discussed the trial before Caesar, which resulted in some hope for reconciliation and even fairness for both father and sons. At the second trial of these two sons, Josephus tells us, Caesar was absent, and in his place were the two presidents of Syria, Saturninus and Volumnius, and an assembly of about 150 magistrates (*Antiquities* XVI.11.2). In this "trial," Herod was clearly in no doubt about his sons' guilt and did not seek a judgment on the matter; instead he came alone and before the assembly made an accusation "very unlike what a father should say about his sons" (*Antiquities* XVI.11.2; Josephus 1969: 355).[1] Josephus describes Herod as being nearly beside himself with rage and open to no persuasion whatsoever.

---

[1] Veyne argues, however, that among the Roman ruling class, of which Herod was clearly a member, "A paterfamilias worthy of the name avoided criticism by soliciting advice from friends and peers, seeking their approval in advance for any important private decision, whether it be to punish a son in accordance with paternal authority or to free a young slave or to marry or to repudiate a wicked wife or to remarry or to commit suicide (for otherwise a suicide might be accused of cowardice) . . . There was no conspiracy of silence within the governing class. Public and private wrongs were set forth for all to see" (1987: 173). Thus Josephus found it "indecent" for Herod to have spoken in an unreasonable and unreasoning fury to the assembly, not for him to have brought his complaints about his sons to a public forum.

No one spoke for the sons, and the sons did not speak for themselves, although they had done so, you will remember, before Caesar. As a result, "the members of the council, being agreed that they were in no position to soften him or effect a reconciliation, confirmed his authority" (*Antiquities* XVI.11.3; Josephus 1969: 357). While some urged lenience, there was an apparent majority in favor of the death penalty for the sons: a penalty, Herod reminded them, he had the right to impose himself even without their concurrence. What, then, is going on here? Is this a trial, or do the "judges" simply confirm the authority of a parent to find his own sons guilty and worthy of the death-sentence?

It is precisely such an ambiguity that confronts sociological observers. When is a trial not a trial? One answer could be that a trial, like the "show trials" in the Soviet Union, is really a staged demonstration of official authority: whether that authority is patriarchal or that of the modern nation-state. As soon as some action is staged, however, it is not clear whether the demonstration is a "mere demonstration" or the enactment of the real thing. A dress rehearsal by a ballet company may be indistinguishable from the real thing and may in fact be a better performance than the one on the "opening night." In the same vein, (but with quite a different illustration in mind), Runciman notes that it is sometimes difficult to distinguish between "watching a rehearsal, or a practical joke, or the making of a film" (1983: 59). The point is that any action may be ambiguous in itself, and that collective actions such as a trial or demonstration may therefore amplify the ambiguity far beyond the capacity of any observer to resolve it by definition.[2]

That is precisely where theory comes in. It is the task of the observer to come up with a theory. In the first place, that theory would enable him or her to know what it is that is being

---

[2] This is not to say that there was something peculiar about the trials of Herod's sons: peculiarly difficult or ambiguous, that is to say. Tacitus makes it clear that "official sharp practices" existed in Rome and made certain individuals suffer terrible prosecution under "preposterous" charges. By such "sharp practices" he has in mind "corruption in the courts, and bullying by advocates, with their continual threats of prosecution" (1956;1988: 91, 93).

described. In the case of the "trial" of Alexander and Aristobulus, for instance, it may well be that we are observing a collective form of producing scapegoats, in which undeserving victims are blamed for the ills of the community and eliminated in an attempt to restore the community's tranquility. Scapegoats, however, are generally chosen somewhat arbitrarily and are usually unattractive because of their age, poverty, illness, or some other disfigurement (Burkert 1987). Alexander and Aristobulus, however, as Josephus frequently reminds us, were well known as fine-looking men with great ability, popularity, and good character. Sacrifice rather than scapegoating, therefore, might be a better term for this collective decision to destroy "the best and the brightest" of Herod's family.

Clearly, it is difficult for the observer to discriminate between a trial, a sacrifice, and the collective production of scapegoats. Of course, the boundaries between these acts usually need clarification: a task of definition that contributes to the building of theory. As Runciman (1983: 62) has observed, however, it is also true that the boundaries between acts may themselves be somewhat obscure. I would note, for instance, that it is quite clear when a liturgy or the signing of a peace treaty or the sitting of a particular court both begins and ends; less formal acts tend to blend into each other.

THE TRIALS OF THE OBSERVER

Why, therefore, not ask people what they think they are doing? On the face of it, this strategy makes sense, and it is appealing for various egalitarian reasons that sometimes inform sociological inquiry. There has indeed been a reaction to the "colonialist" presumptions that allowed sociologists and anthropologists to define (often as irrational behavior) what individuals and groups thought they themselves were doing. Again, partly in response to critiques of scientific reasoning and partly in response to countercultural movements, sociologists have been more willing to blur the line between the observer and the observed. Especially when observing a play or a ceremony, for instance, it is impossible for the audience not to affect the performance or for the observer of a ritual not to be involved in the production of the rite itself: an observation that holds true for less liturgical, more theatrical performances. There is a sense in which the participants in a trial or any other ceremony have the privilege of defining what it is they are doing, but once one inquires of them *what* they are doing, it is almost inevitable that one will be finding out something more, for example, *why* they are doing it. That information, however, belongs under the rubric either of interpretation or of "explanation" (Runciman 1983: 69).

To illustrate how problematical it is to consult the actors about what they are doing, take Josephus' report of another trial: the one in which Antipater is finally brought to what passed at the time for justice. Antipater had been forging letters to implicate Pheroras, Herod's brother, in a plot on Herod's life; he had also been betrayed by correspondence with his mother in which their complicity was revealed. A poisonous potion, presumably intended by Antipater for Herod, had also been discovered, and "the usual suspects" had been rounded up for their testimony (*Antiquities* XVII.4.2). The president-elect of Syria, Varus, was in Jerusalem, and Herod made use of his presence as an assessor and a judge. Although the account of Herod's speech at Antipater's trial before Varus is somewhat abbreviated in the *Antiquities*, where Josephus provides only a summary, Josephus' account in the *Jewish War* provides a long speech by Herod. I turn to it here as a source of some clues as to what Herod, at least, thought he was doing in this trial.[3]

Far from being a show trial, this one was very serious business

---

[3] For a summary of the background to this trial, it would be hard to improve on Cornfeld's precise rendition: "Antipater pursued his course and endeavored to gain a firmer hold on Judaea and strengthen his position in Rome, doing his utmost to enlist the support of Herod's friends there. He was aided in Judaea by his uncle Theudion (*Antiq.* XVII.70) the brother of his mother, who had married Aristobulus' widow, Berenice (*Antiq.* XVII.9), in order to gain support from both Salome and her. In addition, a reconciliation between Antipater and pro-Hasmonean circles was made possible through Antipater's marriage to the daughter of Antigonus, last king of the former dynasty; the children she bore him were no less Hasmonean than the children and grandchildren of Herod and Mariamme (*Antiq.* XVII.92)." It is clear, therefore, that the rivalry between generations was intensified by struggles between the Idumaean and Hasmonean dynasties and their ethnic communities, as I mentioned at greater length in the Introduction.

indeed. Herod begins his speech with the usual protests and complaints that all he seeks is justice: recompense for the injuries received from Antipater and for the many gifts and liberties that Herod had conferred upon him as successor to the throne:

What I fear is that *my* fate may also appear hateful to you and that you may judge me deserving of every calamity for having begotten such sons. And yet you ought rather to pity me for having been the most devoted of fathers to such abominable wretches. (*Jewish War* 1.32.2; Josephus 1927: 295)

There follows a rehearsal of all that Herod had done for Antipater, as if to say that it is only justice that is called for here, with Herod himself being beyond reproach for Antipater's crimes.

None the less, there are indications that something more than justice is to be served. As Herod puts it, it is as if "some evil genius is bent on desolating my house and raising up against me one after another those who are nearest to my heart" (*Jewish War* II.32.2; Josephus 1927: 299). The fates, moreover, require some sacrifice if they are to be propitiated; a larger and more transcendental justice requires the most costly payment, even the life of a son. In Josephus' account in *Antiquities*, it is Caesar's friend and advocate, Nicolaus, who refers to the larger dimension of Antipater's crime.[4] Arguing that "parricide is a wrong done to both nature and humanity," Nicolaus implies that parricide is a form of pollution that must be overcome if the world itself is to be restored to wholeness, since "he who does not punish it does wrong to nature" (*Antiquities* xvII.5.5; Josephus 1927: 427). Antipater has sent out a "venom" into the entire household of Herod and into the society itself; it contaminates everyone, including those who refuse to punish it. Indeed, purification seems to have been the desire of all who testified; everyone purged themselves by speaking out all that they knew of Antipater's plots, while they had remained silent before either out of fear or out of a sense of civility that suspends judgment as long as possible (*Antiquities* xvII.5.6). It would be surprising if

---

[4] It is clear that Josephus relied on the records of Nicolaus, who was also the author of the prosecution speech. See Cornfeld 1982: 118, n.638(a).

such a dramatic trial had not affected the popular imagination of a day of judgment in which the secrets of all hearts are revealed and a society is once again purified of the poisons that afflict it (cf. Matthew 10:26–27).[5]

Clearly the intention here, on Josephus' part, is to convey the impression that speech was at last freed from the constraints of the past, and that there was no more need for deception or any possibility of it.[6] Even Antipater is at a loss for words, and, as is the way with scoundrels, Josephus argues, Antipater appeals to God as witness of his innocence (*Antiquities* xvii.5.6). Once the poisonous potion which Antipater had intended for Herod is given to some unfortunate criminal, it is clear that all doubt has been removed about Antipater's guilt. Language and reality appear to be joined together in a verdict of guilty, and all that needs to be said has been spoken until the last word is uttered.

Even Josephus' account, however, raises doubts about the accomplishment of this trial. Serious business it is, but the account itself leaves me unconvinced that all ambiguity about the trial itself has been removed. In this testimony itself, as I have noted, it is not clear whether justice is being sought or a sacrifice is being offered to the fates in order to restore peace to social life and to repair some horrible offense to nature itself. In Josephus' account in *The Jewish War*, Nicolaus is said to have "launched out into a severe indictment, attributing to him all the crimes which had been committed throughout the realm . . ." (*Jewish War* 1.32.4; Josephus 1927: 303). There is a suggestion here that something more than justice or even sacrifice is going on: something approaching the production of a scapegoat. Indeed, the trial ends without a verdict or a sentence being given; Varus withdraws, consults privately with Herod, and returns to his palace in Syria. Antipater awaits his sentence

---

[5] Against this suggestion should be weighed the observation that Roman habits of governance tended to make domestic secrets public knowledge: Nero publicized his wife's adulteries just as Augustus had made public his daughter's sexual activities. See Veyne 1987: 39.

[6] Note Veyne's reminder that "the Romans washed their dirty linen in public" (1987: 171). In this simple phrase he confirms the argument that I have been making, that the search for purification underlies the desire to establish words beyond a shadow of doubt by discountenancing lies, deception, fakery, and ambiguous or double meanings in public discourse.

in prison. It is hard to know when the trial is over, and whether in fact it was really a trial, or a preliminary to sacrifice, or a particularly crude and obvious production of a scapegoat. In any event, the overtones of the text suggest that a purgative is being applied to the body politic, as if its very health, its ability to reproduce itself, were in question.

As I have noted, it is difficult to know one collective act from another, just as it is sometimes difficult to know a real trial from a show trial. The observer's lot is not unhappy, but it is usually difficult to answer the question, "What is going on here?" Furthermore, if it is not much help to ask people what they think they are doing, how then is an observer to try to resolve the ambiguities I have been discussing without importing theories into his or her report? Josephus' reports, in this case, only compound the difficulty. (Those speeches quoted verbatim at some length in *Antiquities* are merely paraphrased and summarized in *The Jewish War* and vice versa.) There are also some discrepancies of detail: Herod's gift to Antipater for his trip to Rome is reported as 30 talents in one account (*Antiquities*) and 300 in the other (*Jewish War*).

The major ambiguities are due to Josephus' own agenda. I have suggested that Josephus may have constructed his series of reports on the trials of the sons to show how the breakdown of justice, in the increasing absence or distance of Caesar from these hearings of Herod, allows trials to degenerate into forms of sacrifice or scapegoating. The "ritual machinery" of scapegoating becomes more obvious, and even when the defendant, Antipater, is clearly guilty, no fault is found with Herod himself for running an abusive and luxurious regime. Runciman's (1983: 65,69) cautionary remarks about "preemptive theory" hiding within an observer's report are particularly apt in considering these accounts of Josephus, whose own skepticism may have led him to assume that the hearings themselves were primarily for the purpose of legitimating Herod's authority (as in the trial of Alexander and Aristobulus), satisfying his bloodthirsty impulses, managing public impressions (lest anyone think Herod had brought these calamities upon himself), restoring public peace through scapegoating, or swaying

Caesar's own opinion of who was at fault in Palestine. I will return to the question of whether Josephus' report, as a second-hand set of observations, is so informed by his "pre-emptive" notions that one should dismiss it altogether. There may be some basic observations, even if they are informed by his theory, that we can salvage.

His theory, furthermore, is worth considering in its own right. In the introduction I discussed the possibility that Josephus is tracing the causes of the eventual civil war in Palestine and the Romans' destruction of Jerusalem to the crisis of succession from Herod to his sons. The first trial, with Caesar, the personification of transcendent justice present, is clearly a trial, with hope of "equity and reconciliation." The second trial, also of Aristobulus and Alexander, lacks Caesar's presence, although the two surrogates, the presidents of Syria, substitute for Caesar. They, however, see no hope for "equity and reconciliation" and merely confirm Herod's authority. The result is a sacrifice of two young men who represent the ideals of Roman youth and imperial rule. The third trial resembles a scapegoating rite, since the son destined for death (Antipater) is a hideous example of manhood and offends the ideal either of youthful virtues or of just authority; this affair is presided over by Herod, an interested and corrupt party, and Varus, who is yet to assume the authority of the presidency of Syria. The result is the breakdown of legitimate authority, the failure of judicial or quasi-judicial rites to produce transcendent justice, and the opening wide of the crisis in succession.

THEORY EMBEDDED IN OBSERVATION: RELIABILITY VERSUS VALIDITY

Lest the reader should have any doubt about Josephus' theory, Josephus himself records an incident that was contemporary with the trial of Antipater. Just as Herod was contemplating how to give Antipater a public execution, "To his other troubles was now added an insurrection of the populace" (*Jewish War* 1.33.1; Josephus 1927: 307). Two teachers of the Law had attracted a large and growing audience including "quite an army of men in their prime." The teachers apparently heard that "the king was gradually sinking under despondency and disease" (*Jewish War* 1.33.2; Josephus 1927: 309); Josephus portrays them as opportunists, however learned they may have been. Herod's weakness apparently gave them the courage of their convictions, one of which was that "this was the fitting moment to avenge God's honour" (*ibid.*): clearly a rhetorical jab not only at their courage but also at their convictions.

Josephus' assumption here is one of the most difficult biases to overcome in the description of any ritual or public demonstration: an assumption that some of the participants are acting in bad faith. Runciman (1983: 64–65) takes some pains to remind us that a rite is still valid even when performed or attended with varying degrees of faith, and that to assume otherwise is to twist one's report into the shape of a covert explanation. Even the young men, Josephus (*Jewish War* 1.33.3) points out, took heart from a report that Herod was dying: an impurity of nature that does not alter the fundamental right of rebellion. At the suggestion of the learned teachers, and with assurances that they would go to heaven as martyrs if they were caught in the act, the young men removed an eagle from above the great gate of the Temple in an act of good as well as perhaps bad faith.

A symbol of Rome, put there by Herod himself, the eagle offended laws against graven images, rekindled desires for national purity, and stimulated dreams of the return of the nation's power. Herod burned the teachers alive, along with the young men who cut down the eagle; the others were apparently put to a simpler death (*Jewish War* 1.33.3). Josephus' theory is clear enough: that is, that the corruption of imperial justice and the decadence of judicial ritual led to a crisis of succession in which the young men of Israel faced new trials. They, like Herod's sons, carried out the ambitions of the old and paid for their own dreams of glory with their lives. So long as Josephus' reports, however much they may be informed by his own theory, are in themselves acceptable, however, there is no reason to discard the information that they supply.

On the face of it, there is no reason to doubt that there was widespread confusion in Herodian Palestine concerning the question of entitlements. That is clearly Josephus' observation, however much it is informed by Josephus' theory about Caesar as the source of all entitlement. Indeed, Josephus makes it clear that no successor of Herod was entitled to the succession without Caesar's express consent, just as Herod was not entitled to consider himself a friend rather than a subject of Caesar unless Caesar so chose to call him.[7] Neither was Herod entitled to invade Arabia to exact payment for a debt unless authorized to do so by Caesar's representatives, the presidents of Syria; indeed, it was Sylleus' false testimony (that Herod had acted without such authorization) that brought about Caesar's anger toward Herod. Regardless of Josephus' eagerness to demonstrate to his Roman patrons that he subscribed to the imperial theory of entitlements, it is still quite possible that such entitlements were in fact highly suspect, frequently disputed, easily contested, and often claimed as well as lost by a wide range of contenders and pretenders.

In other words, observers have to make decisions about who is entitled to what: young men "entitled" to take down Roman eagles, one son or another "entitled" to the succession to Herod. If those who are being observed are themselves in conflict and doubt about such claims to valid entitlements, however, the observer has a right either to be somewhat vague on the subject or to make decisions that do not "preempt," as Runciman puts it, the actual reporting of events. Josephus may have been right or wrong about his Caesarian theory of entitlements; he is clearly making reports that are informed by that theory. None the less, where is the evidence that the crisis of succession did *not* take place as reported? Where is the evidence that there were *no* corollary events in the streets of Jerusalem; *no* young men making their own grab at the symbols of imperial authority?

These are separate questions from asking, "Who, then, will be the panel of judges to assess these claims to valid entitlements?" (cf. Runciman 1983: 62). The questions about what other

---

[7] There was an institution of friendship in Roman society quite unlike any other that I am aware of; note Veyne's discussion: "The council of friends had something of a formal quality, and in old families when one quarreled with a friend and no longer wanted his presence on the council, it was necessary to notify him officially of that fact (*renuntiare amicitiam*)" (1987: 173).

observers have to say about the crisis of succession or the corresponding events at the Temple are about the "reliability" of Josephus' observations. However, the questions about who will assess or judge the claims of the young to various entitlements are claims about the "validity" of Josephus' judgments.

Problems of reliability and validity are, to the sociologist, what rain, sleet, snow, and dark of night are supposed to be to the postman: no great impediments to the task. It is the observer's task to come up with a theory, and – in this case – it is the twentieth-century sociologist's task to come up with a theory based in part on Josephus' observations. If his observations of the trials of Herod's sons are informed by his assumption that justice is better served in the presence than in the absence of Caesar, it is still possible to use his observations of the trials as ingredients for the sociological task of theory-building *so long as there is no evidence to the contrary*. Were the trials more like show trials, sacrifices, and scapegoating mechanisms the more they were at the disposal of Herod in the absence of Caesar? As Caesar's representatives diminished in stature and number (from two presidents of Syria to one president-elect, as it were), Herod's domination of the proceedings became more complete. In Runciman's terms, one is "free to reject the descriptive presupposition as misconceived while accepting as accurate reports framed in terms which imply, and are meant to imply, that presupposition" (1983: 89). I conclude that it is a fairly reliable observation that the trials of the sons were difficult to distinguish from sacrifices and scapegoating. *After all, we are still in the area of our original problematic: the difficulty a society has in reproducing itself from one generation to the next when faced with the ambiguous and opaque quality of actions and with the difficulty of construing them into acts.*

Now, however, we are talking about actions by corporate actors. These are in effect the acts of a collectivity: that is, the Roman empire or the kingdom of Herod. They are no less problematic for being corporate. Josephus records sometimes what is intended to pass for the direct speech of the participants and sometimes as a paraphrase of their testimony; still, in the absence of conflicting observations, it is possible to adopt a cautious attitude that accepts his transcript of the proceedings as reliable, if not in every detail (for example, the number of talents given to Antipater by Herod). As for the validity of Josephus' judgment that the young were grasping for entitlements (the throne, the eagle) that were not theirs, that is a judgment based on a theory of entitlements: that is, on a set of values. It is not necessary to share those values (deference to age, obedience to Caesar, prohibition of graven images and Roman insignia on the Temple) to treat as valid the judgment that basic entitlements were seriously at issue. The conflict was indeed about who is entitled to what at various ages and under particular conditions.

As a sociological observer I am not bound by Josephus' apparent bias in favor of the entitlements of seniority. It is easy for the sociologist to assume another criterion of validity that neutralizes the claims of the old as well as of the young while trusting Josephus' description of events. As Runciman points out:

in the ordinary case, the use of an evaluative term does not prevent the assertion in question from functioning as a simple report which the rival observer can accept as accurate even if he is wholly out of sympathy with the evaluation presupposed. (1983: 89)

Being a contemporary of the events inside Herod's palace and in the square outside would not necessarily have been a great advantage. Consider the students' uprising in Beijing and their demonstrations during May and June 1989 in Tiananmen Square. There, as in Jerusalem, there was a crisis of succession in party headquarters and a public demonstration focused on symbols in the major square of the capital city. There, as in Jerusalem, the symbols involved the state and the nation: not the eagle and the Temple, but a figure closely resembling the Statue of Liberty. In both cities, separated by nearly two millennia, it was the young who were primarily asserting their political rights against the old (although the crisis of succession in party headquarters involved only sympathies with the young versus the old rather than youthful pretenders to high party office). Both sets of events could be taken as preludes to a civil war. Josephus clearly sees in his events the beginning of the end of the nation; there were also some observers in Beijing who were promoting the notion that civil war was imminent. In both cases the nature of collective actions was problematical. No one could be sure of how widespread was the political support for the students in Beijing, and afterward the more conservative or frightened members of the population distanced themselves from the students. In Jerusalem also, when Herod called for the execution of the Rabbis and young men who removed the eagle from the Temple gate, large numbers of the population were quick to dissociate themselves from the culpable few. Clearly a local panel of judges would have had difficulty in deciding the validity of various claims to entitlement in the public squares both of Jerusalem and of Beijing as well as at party headquarters and Herod's palace. Clearly also rival explanations for the events would have informed every report of dissidence and incipient civil war, and some of the prophecies may indeed have been self-fulfilling. The observations that are available from Beijing owe a great deal to the highly selective focus of the mass media (which concentrated on a brave young man confronting a tank rather than on citizens beating soldiers to death). Josephus' observations are no less selective in their focus, but that does not affect their reliability any more than the media's selection of the young man in front of the tank suggests that the event itself was contrived. The task of the observer remains the same in each case: to develop a theory out of observations that are already embedded in accounts informed by others' assumptions, values, and implicit explanations of the events themselves.

Even if it were possible to interview the young men who took down the Roman eagle in Jerusalem or who erected the Statue of Liberty in Beijing, the interviews themselves might not be very revealing. In both cases it may well be that the individuals themselves did not know entirely why they were performing these provocative acts of symbolic protest and rebellion. It is possible that the hostility of the young men toward older patriarchs was displaced in both cases on to these symbols. It is also possible that the young men had murderous thoughts or even intentions regarding the old; parricide did not begin or end in the Palestine of the first century. If the young men did harbor such parricidal motives, it is also possible, even likely, that on some unconscious level they felt that they should pay for the imagined crimes. Under these conditions it is possible that the young men were willing to risk their lives since death would be a punishment fitting for the fantasied crime of parricide. The young men in Beijing who started the demonstration were in fact risking death through a long fast. In other words, suicidal motives, along with parricidal ones, may have been widely shared among a network of youths in both situations, and the events in the public squares simply dramatized the murderous undercurrents of inter-generational conflict in the larger society and in the state itself. Such a theory of "collective neurosis" could well inform Josephus' account; in fact he dwells on the collective suicidal aspects of the civil war itself and calls them "madness." Whether or not he is right, we "should be prepared to accept as a term of reportage even a term pre-emptive of a theory . . . generative of invalid explanatory hypotheses" so long as it is clear to what the term refers (Runciman 1983: 90). The civil war may not have been the result of a collective drive toward national suicide; none the less the possibility of suicidal motives among the young males of Palestine suggests that the term collective neurosis refers to real, however unconscious – and therefore difficult to observe – motives of rebellion and parricide.

In building a theory, furthermore, the observer has the right to develop some scaffolding: a structure on which to get to work face to face, as it were, with the building itself. Take, for example, the corporate acts with which this chapter has been engaged. They can be arranged along a dimension from the most clear to the most problematic. In the trial before Caesar, the nature of the justice to be served is relatively clear, but the second trial of Alexander and Aristobulus was more like the sacrifice of idealized young men to restore an authority that was essential to the continuation of the social system, however compromised that authority may have been by Herod's paranoia. The third trial was more like a scapegoating mechanism to cure a system of all its ills, however guilty was the party delivered over to sentencing and execution. The public demonstration continues to increase the level of ambiguity and raise the level and scope of violence; in it the problematic nature of collective action follows out the earlier focus on problematic corporate acts in the trials of the sons. Later in Josephus these collective acts become increasingly ambiguous, puzzling, and self-destructive, until the city itself is lost in fire, insurrection, and punitive Roman revenge. The causes and ends of the conflict become increasingly vague and problematical along this same continuum, and therefore the difficulties of explanation and evaluation are also compounded. Even motives become more obscure, as the possibilities for self-deception and self-destruction become more evident from one end of this spectrum to the other. One dimension or spectrum for our analysis, then, is the degree of ambiguity in the motives, causes, functions, and ends of corporate and collective acts (see matrix 1).

A second dimension for our analytic scaffolding is the level of analysis. In earlier chapters we have focused on individual actors and on actors in roles. Here we are focusing on a network of roles: sons in relation to fathers both within their own households and outside in the larger society. The network extends, therefore, from the most immediate, direct, face to face and relatively closed, as in the case of the sons of Herod, to the more extended network of roles that brings the young male "youth" of the nation into contact with representatives of the law: Rabbis speaking for the laws of the nation that prohibit graven images, but also the Temple garrison that imposes the law of the kingdom on the youths who took part in the demonstration of contempt for the Roman eagle. The spectrum can be continued outward, however, to include a more diffuse and open set of relationships among youths who are united to each other only by the most diffuse ties of kinship and national loyalty: the young men of Israel whose network may be relatively open and permeable to outside influences when compared with the young men who were "disciples" of the Rabbis. These latter young men are potential recruits for an

Matrix 1. *Degree of ambiguity in entitlements (rights) claimed by youths*

	Degree of ambiguity in social acts	
	Low	High
Level of analysis Roles encapsulated	1. Rights clear	2. Rights implicit
Roles open-ended	3. Rights explicit	4. Rights vague

insurrection, but they are dispersed in a variety of regions and among various occupations, and derive from a larger set of households and lineages. They could be recruited as well by prophetic movements as by guerilla leaders, and they are part of a larger sociological category, "youth," and not merely members of the more restricted categories of son and disciple. Societal control over these youths is relatively low, therefore, since their network is relatively open and complex while their collective acts would be relatively difficult to define. Above I discussed two tribes (the Melpa and the Etero among New Guinea Highlanders) who were quite different along precisely this spectrum: that is, in openness to outsiders and in willingness to engage in exchange with foreigners. It was the most encapsulated tribe, you will remember, who had the greatest fears of being drained and who were most likely to be filled with fears of pollution from outside influences.

At one end of the spectrum or dimension, then, are young males whose lives are relatively encapsulated within a household, defined by ties of kinship and social status within a particular family, and relatively uniform in age, education, opportunities for mobility, and in occupational status and achievement. Their gestures of obedience and deference – or of disobedience and insurrection – are relatively easy to define, and their being encapsulated in the family or local community further enables the society to exercise high levels of control over them. They are far more easily defined as dangerous and more quickly convicted than the youths at the other end of the spectrum whose lives are far less uniform, whose statuses are less clearly defined, and whose lives, being less encapsulated by family and local communities, exhibit wider variations in achievement and life-chances. In the contrast between these two conditions, for instance, might be seen the very different fates of the youths who tore down the eagle from over the Temple gate and the relatively young men who, leaving their parents' occupations, may have joined a variety of religious and protest movements in the towns and cities of the provinces.

FROM MODEL TO THEORY-BUILDING

There is something to be gained by ranging so many actors along a spectrum like this. The spectrum displays some of the differences that individuals may have who are none the less united by a single status or set of characteristics: young males. The level of analysis is thus raised somewhat higher than the notion of sons implies: we are asking what young men whose lives are defined by being someone's sons, for example, the sons of Herod or the son of Joseph and Mary, have in common with those whose lives are defined by being members of a category, that is, young men. This level of analysis requires us to ask the same questions of all of them: Whom do they know? Can they communicate with strangers? Are they open to influences from outside the home, the community, the religious group, and even the nation? Are they at the disposal of a despotic patriarch, or do they have opportunities to leave the family and even the region? These questions were vital to the survival of Herod's sons; they were also vital to the lives, the opportunities, and eventually even to the survival of young men in the nation as Israel became mobilized for insurrection and split by a civil war. At stake, analytically speaking, is what Runciman calls the "control of the roles which children (and very often women) may occupy and control of the definition of kinship itself" (1983: 102). In a society based on house and lineage, to control the definition of kinship, I would add, makes it possible to control the symbolic reproduction of the society itself.

Now, how can the observer use this scaffolding to begin to erect a theory? Imagine the two dimensions as if they cut across each other. One dimension is still the degree of ambiguity in corporate acts; that dimension extends from the trial which is relatively coherent and complete, through sacrifice and scape-goating to demonstrations and insurrections that are relatively and progressively incomplete, ambiguous, and therefore more difficult to describe, interpret, and explain. The other end of the spectrum from the trial is the breakdown of the collectivity in civil war. Cutting across this dimension is our level of analysis, which extends from the relatively closed and coherent network of the sons of a single household, for example, Herod's, to the relatively open and ambiguous network of young males of the region and even of the nation itself.

Our notions of what we are observing are therefore relatively simple: corporate acts involving relatively closed or open networks of young men. The sociological ground (the levels of analysis) that we are attempting to cover, however, is very broad. It begins with the hapless sons of Herod and other young men encapsulated in the household and the local community, whose every gesture is immediately coded and decoded for signs of subversion. Under these conditions (cell 1 of matrix 1) controls are of course excruciatingly high. The model includes the more ambiguous controls exercised over young men whose network of roles may be relatively encapsulated but whose collective acts may be more ambiguous and also collectively defined with implicit understandings about the rights even of the poor but literate in the Torah to challenge adult authority (cell 2). These young dissidents may therefore be collectively defined as zealous, learned in the Torah, and disputatious over the Law. No doubt this avenue permitted greater degrees of freedom as well as of ambiguity in the nature of social acts and corresponding weakness of social control. Other young men may have engaged in pilgrimages that turned into insurrections; over them control was somewhat less ambiguous, since, al-though they had been liberated from the immediate control of the family and the local community by assuming the role and prerogative of the pilgrim, they were engaged in collective acts of relatively well-defined devotion and duty (cell 3): for example, attendance at the rites of the Passover or Pentecost. As these rites failed to contain collective passions, however, and turned into riots and rebellion, these youths may well have been recruited by wandering prophets or guerilla leaders and engaged in acts of relative freedom, with rights that are relatively ambiguous and immune to social control (cell 4).

The purpose of this analytical scaffolding is to enable the observer to inspect more closely the world that he or she is intent on examining. Suppose, for instance, that you are an observer in a position roughly analogous to cell 4 of the matrix. You would be examining the network of young males in a region who are potential participants in demonstrations, insurrections, guerilla movements, and perhaps even civil war. What would you expect to find, for instance, to replace the trial as a means of defining entitlements and settling disputes over the nature of social acts? In the place of a single source of legitimate political authority one would expect to find many claimants to the right to speak with authority. Instead of a single trial that defines the rights of sons, one would perhaps find a series of tests, one after another, in which the young men seek to demonstrate their powers *vis-à-vis* the older men of the region or nation. Where one finds families set against each other, with sons denouncing fathers and fathers denouncing sons, and with others in the same family likewise turning against each other, there will indeed be calls for a day of judgment: for tests to settle, once and for all, competing and conflicting claims to entitlements.

As I have already noted, what is at stake is the control of patriarchs over the roles of women and children. The more confined and closed their network, the more likely it is that patriarchal authority will be able to define the roles of women and children and to limit their opportunities. Of course, there is a logical possibility that, even in tightly controlled households, there will be demonstrations or even insurrections. Indeed, Herod was sensitive to demonstrations of independence and self-confidence by his sons, and he remained fearful of insurrection in his household; hence his reliance on the methods of social control more typical of cell 1 in matrix 2: i.e. scapegoating, sacrifice, and the trial itself.

Of course, life is seldom static, and networks of roles grow over time as the young mature and develop associations outside the immediate control of the household. The more open and complex the network of sons, the less control will patriarchal authority be able to exert over their roles, as well as over the roles of other children and of women. Under the conditions of a fairly open network (cell 3), even Herod's sons would be open to the influence of outsiders: for example, spies and travelers who became guests of the household. One should not ignore the influence, in the case of Herod's sons, of their Roman education and friends at Caesar's court, as well as the influences of powerful in-laws, such as the king of Syria, Archelaus. Others outside Herod's household also lived under the conditions of a relatively fluid and open network; their sons, and women and children also, could be open to the influence of traveling prophets and evangelists, strangers passing through on business or on pilgrimage, and open also to the more or less powerful suggestions presented by Hellenistic games, theater, and local customs in the cities developed by Herod: that is, not only Jerusalem but the new cities of the provinces where Herod managed to juxtapose both Jews and gentiles in a context like the Greek *polis*, with a central square, a theater, a court or tribunal residence, a treasury and government archives (Cornfeld et al. 1982).

Under these conditions (cell 3), there would be ample opportunities for demonstrations and insurrections: Josephus' record of the years prior to the civil war is full of them. Some of them were inspired by religious leaders, while others were inspired by political and military leaders. All had in common, however, the desire to put their claims to the test: charismatic leadership, as Weber reminded us, is sufficiently unsure of its own prowess to require constant testing, whether in miracles, economic success, or on the field of battle. It is not surprising that the authorities would adopt as countermeasures attempts to scapegoat prophets or guerilla leaders, to offer the best and the brightest as sacrifices, or to bring them to trial.

As corporate acts become less coherent and complete, words and deeds become more problematic; what is said and done in insurrections and civil war requires far more interpretation and explanation than the clear, complete, and final sentence of a judge at a well-tried case in the highest court in the land. Compare, for example, the claims of Herod's sons and heirs to assume the kingship of Israel with the popular, prophetic claims of sons and heirs to the kingdom of Israel. There were clearly a number of pretenders to the kingship, some of them in various prophetic movements, others clearly ready for a test of arms. The ambiguity of their claims to the title is a centerpiece of the Synoptic Gospels, and there is no lack of literature on the multiplicity of prophets and messianic leaders of the period. Our problematic, however, focuses on only one aspect of these movements: the ambiguous, contestable, inflated, and often suddenly deflated nature of these claims to entitlement. The question, "By what authority do you do these things?" under-scores the problematic aspects of claims to authority, kingly or otherwise. It also suggests that there may have been a wide-spread demand for someone who could speak and act with incontrovertible authority.

Another aspect of the model in matrix 2 suggests some of the logical possibilities of our investigation into ambiguous and questionable words and deeds. Even in the tightly confined network of Herod's sons, there was relatively little difference of opinion as to the meaning of the term son. Ambiguity increased with the use of the term heir, of course, since not all Herod's sons were to be heirs, and not all heirs were to share equally in the inheritance. Ambiguity about the meaning of the terms son and heir increased, however, as the network of young males became more complex, open, and extended. In fact, as Runciman (1983: 102) notes, the nature of kinship itself comes into question. Any reader familiar with the Synoptic Gospels can come up with several illustrations of discussions about the nature of kinship: Jesus himself refusing to define his brothers and sisters in terms of blood relationships. The "true" nature of kinship becomes as problematical, therefore, as the entitlements of sons and daugh-ters, of women and children. Under the conditions suggested by cell 4, then, we would expect to find public discourse and private instruction focusing on the ambiguity of what it means to be a son and heir, a brother or sister. Kinship itself becomes so broad a term as to suggest a whole new range of entitlements for those who are "brothers of the sons of Man."

If it is the task of the observer to come up with a theory, part of that task is, of course, one of description. A good theory will enable one to know what one ought to expect to find under certain conditions: that is, to anticipate what there will be to report. In this chapter I have focused entirely on the task of description in order to suggest some of the analytical steps that are involved in mapping out the social terrain. Any such map, of course, will oversimplify what is to be found "on the ground," so to speak; the map itself may so distort social reality that it becomes an impediment and must be discarded.

You will note that nothing in this chapter has touched on the *interpretation* of life under these various conditions. We have not been asking what it would be like to live, for instance, in a world where the entitlements of sons were in continual dispute or where the notion of kinship was being stretched beyond any recognizable or previous limits. In the same interpretive vein, we have not been looking at the corollaries of such confusion in other areas of social life, although I was suggesting that authority in business and on the battlefield might also be "up for grabs," unsure of itself, and all too ready for confirmation not in a legal trial but in a test of prowess in gaining wealth or using arms. Display was seldom merely ornamental, and it often served the purpose of laying to rest any doubts that others might have had of the individual's wealth or power. More important- ly, however, we have not discussed the corollaries of scapegoat- ing and sacrifice outside the household of Herod: the many forms in which sons were placed at the mercy – and the disposal – of patriarchs in antiquity. These related forms of social life are the subject of our next chapter.

CHAPTER 5

The search for useful concepts: evil and charisma

REVIEWING THE ARGUMENT: SUCCESSION CRISES BREED DREAD AND DESPAIR

In this chapter I wish to expand on the question, "What is it like to live in a society that is suffering from a crisis in succession?" That crisis, as we have seen, affects the choice of "The king of the Jews": a title with which Pilate honored, however mockingly, the messianic figure from Galilee. In so doing Pilate gives us an additional reason for thinking that the crisis of succession and the choice of a legitimate "king of the Jews" was still endemic and unresolved in Israel three or more decades after the death of Herod. The crisis in succession also affects the relation of one age-set to another, that is, of sons to fathers, and thus raises issues about the meaning or necessity of sons "being about their fathers' business."

As I argued in chapter 1, the succession in a patrilineal society must go smoothly if that society is to continue to believe in its ability to own and control the sources of life. If the society in question is going to reproduce itself, sons must succeed fathers, and kings-designate must succeed the former ruler. That process of reproduction occurs, however, in many spheres: in the fertility of the fields, in the deference of the young to the old, in success in hunting or in agriculture, in mining or in manufacture, in the martial or in the fine arts. The issue in each case is the same, that is, that the vitality of the society depends on the succession of one generation and of one regime to another. A society whose vitality is in question leads its members into a sense of despair: a haunting and increasingly palpable awareness that the promises of future and abundant life will never be realized.

More is at stake in the process of succession than a society's capacity to feel alive and confident of its ability to reproduce itself. The threat of death itself must also be laid to rest. That threat comes, as I argued in chapter 1, not only from the more obvious and literal dangers posed by enemies, animals, illness, and domestic violence. It also comes from the sources of symbolic opposition to the structure of the society itself. You will remember that in a patriarchal society, women and sexuality are two such sources of opposition. In a society closed to outsiders, intermarriage with women of other communities, like exchange with outsiders, poses a very real threat to the society itself. The more the society relies on strict controls of individual behavior, the more it will see in sexuality and in individuality sources of opposition that threaten the community with the death of its controls and traditions. Societies that are unable to ward off such threats from various sources of opposition tend to inspire a sense of dread: fear and suspicion that an evil will come which will in fact put an end to the social world as people know it.

It has been one of the functions of religion to alleviate the burden of dread and of despair. To put it more positively, religion has functioned to insure, on the one hand, a continual supply of the sources of life and of vitality for societies. For a succession to go on from one generation to the next, the young must pay their dues to the old. Again, for a society to manage the succession from one regime to the next, it is necessary for the new ruler to pay his or her dues to the people, just as it is necessary for the people to pay their dues to the ruler in the form of acclamation, or in promises to pay taxes and other forms of tribute. To make sure, on the other hand, that a society can hold at bay its sources of opposition, religion must ensure that the symbolic or real threat (for example, from individuality) is reduced through various forms of payment: tribute, penance, sacrifice, and confession, to name only the most obvious forms. To forestall a day of reckoning in the contest with opposing forces, religion must control not only untrammeled individuality and sexuality but other forces of destruction, that is, of evil, whether in the form of sickness, mortal enemies, or death itself.

Our question, then, concerns the extent to which religion could inspire such confidence in Israel during the time of Herod and especially in the days preceding his death. Herod was "cruel to all alike and one who easily gave in to anger and was contemptuous of justice" (*Antiquities* XVII.8.1; Josephus 1969: 459): a Stalin or a Hitler, who like them had systematically exterminated the sources of opposition among his friends and enemies; he had also killed wantonly those who were either neutral or among his allies, whether out of fear and hatred or from his suspicions, which grew more intractable with age and sickness. In his last days he ordered that the male leadership of the Jews be incarcerated in the hippodrome, to be murdered at his death, so that national mourning would attend his own funeral. In addition to inviting death and imposing it on the nation, his massive program of Hellenization also threatened Israel's ownership and control of the sources of life. He was a Hellenistic king as well as king of the Jews, and his programs of building Hellenistic cities, of introducing Hellenistic sports, theater, and games into Palestinian culture, and enriching his kingdom at the expense of the Jews not only polarized the Jewish and gentile populations but threatened the ability of the nation to guarantee its own economic, social, and political survival.

It is therefore not surprising to find at Herod's death a crisis of succession not only for the regime and the kingdom but for the nation itself. In this crisis the entitlements of both the king and people were immediately at issue: the king's entitlement to tribute, to acclamation, and to taxes from the people; the people's entitlement to guarantees from the king that he would free prisoners, lower taxes, and pay retribution for the deaths of certain Rabbis and men who had taken down Herod's Roman eagle from the gate of the Temple. Josephus' account is very telling.

At issue is the relation of language to reality, that is, whether threats and promises, testimonies and confessions, can be taken seriously. Note that the distance between the ruler and the ruled has been slightly weakened; Archelaus has not yet been legitimated by Caesar and is therefore most dependent for the time being on the good-will of the people. In some tribes, of course, such a moment is more dramatic, the relationship temporarily more equal, and the demands of the people more theatrical or severe. Turner (1969) recounts the practice in one community of tying the chief-designate to a tree while the people circle him, insult him, and warn him never to forget that he is really just one of them. The temporary equality of presidential candidates with the people in the United States facilitates not only the exchange of information and of promises, but the sense that the means of life will flow easily throughout the entire community for the enrichment of all. At the same time pledges are made between the ruler-to-be and the ruled to defend the community against the sources of opposition from within and without and thus to score significant victories over death. In this way both despair and dread are overcome in dramatic displays of solidarity and resolution, *so long as both the leaders and the people can be taken at their word.*

In the subsequent exchanges between Archelaus and the people, however, religion failed to provide a symbolic victory over death or to renew commitment to build up the common-wealth. On the contrary, the people who came to celebrate the Passover, that ancient victory over death, end up in flight, with over three thousand of them being slaughtered by Archelaus' soldiers. Josephus' (*Antiquities* xvii.9) account reveals that some were still demanding retribution for the death of Matthias (a teacher of the Law who had urged the removal of the Roman eagle from the Temple gate) "and his followers who had been put to death by Herod but because of the fear inspired by him, had at that time been deprived of the honour of being mourned" (*Antiquities* xvii.9.1; Josephus 1969: 467). Note the emphasis on the religious demand to pay respect to the dead through proper mourning. It is as if the society itself could not continue without the payment of the appropriate verbal dues from the living to the dead. That is precisely the point: religion facilitates and requires the payment of certain dues if life is to go on and death to be avoided or overcome.

On the one hand, then, the succession required of the people that they paid their respects to Archelaus. As Josephus notes, however, "the people were altogether more submissive to their

own will than to the authority of their rulers": a willfulness that
threatened to prevent the succession from occurring at all
(*Antiquities* XVII.9.2; Josephus 1969: 469). There could be no
such payment to the successor of Herod, after all, until that
successor allowed the proper payment of the debt of respect and
mourning for those whom Herod had slain. The succession thus
became a crisis because the nation could not get its liturgical act
together. Because the usual transactions between a chief-
designate and the people, as well as the Passover and the rites of
mourning for those killed by Herod were suspended, the
continuity of the nation itself was interrupted. The blessings of
the dead upon the living, of dead fathers on their sons, could
neither be given nor received. Without them, the spiritual
succession of the nation itself was impoverished and in jeopardy.
Until the proper *words* are spoken, such a crisis will continue
unresolved.

RELIGIOUS REMEDIES FOR DREAD AND DESPAIR: THE SYMBOLIC PAYMENT OF DEBTS

One hypothetical answer, then, to the question of what it is like
to live in a crisis of succession is that the people experience a
diffuse, and at times acute, sense of dread and despair. They
despair that what they are entitled to from the nation and its
institutions will not be paid them; they dread that they will be
called upon to pay their debts of tribute and tithe, taxation or
other entitlements even to the uttermost farthing, as it were. In
this climate various schemes may flourish for the liquidation of
debts and for a year of redemption that absolves all forms of
indebtedness. Even these religious solutions, however, impose
new duties and require fresh commitments and reserves of duty
and devotion. Debt is recycled and minted again under fresh
auspices.

How, then, does religion cause, express, relieve, or perpetuate
despair and dread? In a brief essay on method, of course, it is not
possible to answer that question. In fact, it would require a
separate book on theory-construction to show how various
answers could be put forward: each of them fit for guiding

Matrix 2. *Types of social entitlements (debts)*

	Duration of relationships	
	Long	Short
Type of relationship		
Horizontal	1	2
Vertical	3	4

inquiry into the textual and archaeological resources. Here, however, it may be helpful briefly to expand on the notion of entitlements introduced in the last chapter. Here, then, I will sketch out the range of duties and the type of debt that may be found within a single society.

Matrix 2 suggests that debts may be of a long-term or short-term nature. Among the long-term debts may be numbered those owed by the living to the dead and by one generation to another; like the debts of a people to a king whose term is for life, these long-term debts require payments in the form of sacrifice, especially when the relationships are vertical, and therefore both asymmetrical and irreversible (as in cell 3). However, where the relationships are horizontal, long-term debts also may be incurred, for instance, among those taking vows of fidelity, as in marriage or in sororities and fraternities. Under these conditions payments may take the form of an exchange of vows and gifts: promises, blood, rings, the sharing of food, and other tokens of permanent commitment among equals (as in cell 1).

When relationships are relatively short-term, as among nomadic tribes, it is understandable therefore that the death rites should be relatively unceremonious with minimal forms of payment: hardly sacrifice, but rather a symbolic breaking of an object like a gourd, which can then be left on the deceased's grave as the tribe move on (Middleton 1982: 188ff.). As Middleton notes, there is no apparent fear of the dead person's return, and the offering is not inspired, therefore, by dread of his or her presence. I would suggest, then, that dread is heightened in the circumstances indicated by cell 3 (vertical, long-term relationships) and minimized in the conditions I have just mentioned, where even the dead are remembered with a minimum of ceremony and the most modest of payments of respect (cell 4). Where payments are made among equals in short-term relationships (cell 2), of course, the exchanges will be equally modest and the ceremony minimal. As Middleton notes,

an immediate-return system is one in which activity oriented directly to the present . . . is stressed, in which people use their labour to obtain food and other resources which are consumed on the day they are obtained or casually over the days that follow, in which there is a minimum of investment in the long-lasting artifacts or in long-enduring debts, obligations, or other binding commitments to specific kinsmen, affines, contractual partners or to members of bounded corporate groups, however these are recruited. The emphasis is on joint participation in and sharing with an ad hoc local community, undifferentiated except by age and sex, and more generally on ad hoc pragmatism rather than on planning of continuity. (1982: 205–206)

One thinks of Haight-Ashbury, Woodstock, or the other settings of the 1960s in which young people gathered precisely in such ad hoc communities; there the necessities of life flowed with easy mutuality, i.e. whatever food and clothing were available for sharing, without the promises and vows associated with gift-exchange in communities expecting long-term commitments.

Let us return now to the problem of succession. It is clear that the people of Israel would undertake no new debt to the Herodian monarchy until they felt they had paid their debts to the dead. That is, until proper mourning had been offered, as was due to the many whom Herod had killed and especially to those recently murdered for their part in removing the eagle from the Temple, there would be no fresh infusions of moral capital on which the monarchy could draw. The regime and the nation faced a crisis in social credit; there were entitlements that had to be honored before the new regime could go on. What, then, was it like to live at a time of such stalemate, when life could not go on until some terrible debt had been paid by the living to the dead? The search for an answer, I will argue, requires us to introduce the concept of evil.

EVIL

By evil I mean a source of opposition to social life that is sufficient to undermine the social order in its entirety. That is why evil is so often referred to as a destructive force that can dissolve the ties that bind a community together. For instance, in studying the records of Earls Colne from the fifteenth to the eighteenth century, Alan MacFarlane (1985: 63) found that "evil doers" were those who had "failed to pay their debts"; I would add that they were "evil doers" because they had not lived up to their word: they had opened a gap between language and reality that had to be filled with the proper, judicial, sentences. As MacFarlane (1985: 62) notes, the phrase "evil doers" in the fifteenth century gave way to "evil persons" in the eighteenth; these were persons "who had fled to avoid paying their debts."

These cases fall within the generic meaning of evil as defaulting on one's word, whether by withholding payment of debts and duties, tributes and sacrifices or by failing to make proper confessions and penances: that is, failing to honor whatever entitlements are due and necessary if the life of the society is to continue uninterrupted by the succession of generations despite the threat posed by enemies and by death itself.

Now, it matters whether one is looking at "evildoing" or "evil persons," that is, at actions or at individuals. Societies may draw on a wide range of symbols to signify what is problematical about the nature of debts. The sources of opposition may come from actions that are construed as evil acts, but a society's ability to construe individual actions as social acts depends on the strength of its institutions. Certain institutions are indeed supposed to do just that: that is, a society's courts and tribunals, its trials and liturgies construe actions into acts.

Similarly, a society can find its sources of opposition in persons rather than in acts, but its ability to define certain persons as evil depends on its ability to distinguish between an individual and his or her actions. When the individual as a social institution, as a cluster of rights and duties, becomes separate from the individual as an incumbent of a particular status, it is then possible for a society's courts to locate the source of evil in the individual as a social institution opposed to other institutions. If MacFarlane's study can be taken as a guide, the individual as a social institution may have emerged in Earls Colne somewhere between the fifteenth and the eighteenth century. All I am saying at this point, however, is simply that the experience of evil in any community depends on that community's ability to make certain distinctions. That ability in turn depends on a society's complexity, for example, on whether it can distinguish social acts from particular actions or individuals from the statuses which they occupy.

The notion that an unpaid debt can be the source of an unhealthy or unholy opposition within a society is clearly part of the Faustian myth. The debt is created by a verbal promise made to the devil himself. Other myths recall an unpaid debt to the gods: King Minos' debt to Poseidon, who had given Minos a perfect bull for sacrifice; Minos, however, offered up a lesser bull in its stead and kept Poseidon's gift for himself. The unpaid debt was his undoing, as Minos' wife seduced the perfect bull and gave birth to the Minotaur, a destructive force that devoured the young people of Athens. As the image of the Minotaur suggests, there is an animal-like nature that can mingle with the human and so destroy the continuity between generations and a society's ability to reproduce itself. It is the world of nature, so to speak, that opposes and can destroy a society when the proper tribute and sacrifices are not made. The origin of evil is not money but debt.

Indeed, MacFarlane goes on to argue that in peasant societies, notably those of Europe, evil takes on the most threatening aspects and becomes a pervasive source of opposition to social life: like nature itself. MacFarlane (1985: 66) reports that in the small world of Earls Colne the devil had appeared to a man in the form of a bull. I would suggest that in societies that are less differentiated from the natural world and most dependent on its rhythms and vagaries, evil will be symbolized in natural forms which, like the bull, are only partly domesticated and can be very disruptive. Again, the image of evil depends on the distinctions that a society can make, and these in turn depend partly on its complexity, but evil emerges when a gap opens up between words and deeds, language and reality, and threatens the continuation of a society from one generation to the next.

Imagine, then, a social world that is still closely intertwined with the natural order. The same spirits that inhabit humans can inhabit pigs or other animals: note, for instance, the Gadarene demoniac, whose evil spirit, once exorcised by Jesus, drove an entire herd of pigs to their destruction (Luke 8: 26–39). In such a world, where debts are long-term and the distinction between nature and society difficult to draw, the remedy for evil is often in the form of powerful speech: for example, exorcism and purges, through which the body politic, as well as the body of the individual, undergoes a purifying catharsis. Exorcisms cancel, as it were, the debt to nature and free the individual from being "beholden" to natural forces; I use the antique expression because it conveys the same sense of indebtedness precisely.[1] Freud puts it with the same precision when he speaks of an unpaid and universal debt to Eros, that is, to free-floating and unbounded desire for a quasi-natural unity with others. Unsatisfied desire is indeed a perennial source of debt in a social world that can never be wholly separate from nature precisely because human nature takes part in both.

[1] It is interesting to note, for instance, that this healing of the Gadarene demoniac follows (except for a brief interruption) an account that concerns the entitlements of the Pharisees (Luke 7: 30–50). In this account, sins and debts are forgiven, to the consternation of those who, like the Pharisees, have a relatively high view of their own entitlements. (No doubt the connection between the cancellation of debts, healing, and exorcism is typical of the Synoptic Gospel writers.) The methodological concerns that I have developed suggest that there may be a form of sociological interpretation that can link these various aspects of social life (indebtedness, sickness, and so forth) together and can explore, in doing so, the question of what it is like to live in a period in which entitlements, debts, and demands for payment were causing an unhealthy mixture of despair and dread in the general population. This same combination of concerns for entitlement and a day of reckoning is typical, I have suggested, of a society undergoing a succession-crisis. In Israel these concerns may have stimulated demands for a "king of the Jews" who could indeed guarantee the ability of the society to pay its debts, satisfy both the living and the dead, provide for the continuity of the generations, and overcome all sources of contradiction and death itself.

SUMMARY

Societies undergoing a crisis in succession do so at several levels. Certainly the kingship is involved, where succession determines the continuity of the social system and, in some societies, the virtues and health of both the people and the land. The crisis is also felt throughout a patriarchal system, since patriarchy depends for its legitimacy on the ability to keep the flow of life moving from one generation to the next. The succession-crisis within a patriarchy, moreover, engenders conflicts especially between fathers and sons and among brothers, but also more generally between parents and children and among in-laws, as I noted in the previous chapter. Where the generations come into conflict, of course, the question of entitlements is raised in its most acute form, but that question also sharpens relationships between all those in authority and their constituencies, as well as between the relatively rich and the relatively poor.

Once the question of entitlements has been raised, the succession-crisis is felt at still another level, that is, in the form of conflict over the payment of debts and dues, tributes and taxes: indeed, conflict over all forms of indebtedness. The satisfaction of these debts, of course, often depends on the commitments made during certain rites and ceremonies, for example, inaugurations, anointments, and high festivals in which the nation as a whole sanctifies its own commitments and debts both to the living and to the dead. When these rites fail, I have argued, pressures intensify on the words and gestures of everyday life to bear the weight of social honors, of deference and of prescribed demeanor. When these pressures intensify on ordinary conversations, of course, social networks close for the sake of protection from increased surveillance. That is why, for instance, Jesus is reported to have been under such constant scrutiny for his behavior toward those who seemed least entitled to receive the favors he granted them. The succession-crisis thus reaches down into families, to dinner-table conversation, and to greetings on the street, as well as to even more unguarded moments among what may have been believed to be a closed network of trusted associates.

Remember, of course, that the analysis that I have just summarized may be quite off the mark when it comes to describing, let alone to interpreting and explaining, what was actually going on in Palestinian society prior to the civil war of 66–70 CE. The point of any sociological method is to produce an account that can be verified and challenged by rival observers, interpreters, and theorists with some degree of consensus on the rules and means for doing so. Here I have simply taken the observation of disturbed and deceptive communication during such highly significant acts as a trial, especially of the sons of Herod, as a starting point for asking what may be revealed in such a moment at various levels in the Palestinian social system of the period. I have suggested that a succession-crisis appears at each of the levels that I have enumerated in the previous paragraphs.

In addition, I have suggested that the crisis is compounded by the close association of Palestinian society with nature, which requires drastic forms of purification if the debts are to be cancelled. The forms of indebtedness are further complicated by the fact that Palestinian society was not a self-contained social system but overlapped at various levels with the Roman system. That overlapping made all actions even more difficult to construe into acts, all words more problematical and speech more veiled, while making the question of entitlements politically sensitive in the extreme.

In analyzing the strained relationship between language and reality at each of these levels, of course, I am only beginning to develop an explanation: a proto-typical theory. Certainly such an explanation does not constitute a real theory until it can be shown to be part of a more encompassing account of how societies function or fail to function. In addition, it is not much good as a theory unless it can be opposed by countertheories that challenge it succinctly and quite particularly. I will only be able to hint at alternative theories in the epilogue.

In this chapter, moreover, I have been trying to elaborate slightly on what it may have been like to live in a society afflicted by a succession-crisis at so many levels of its existence. The concept that I have suggested, "evil," refers partly to forms of indebtedness and partly to a sense of dread and despair. Dread of being called upon to pay what one owes, and despair of receiving what one is entitled to, constitute a pervasive experience in societies undergoing a crisis in their ability to reproduce themselves. The payment of all sorts of debt thus becomes intensely significant and problematical. That is at least the direction of the argument that I have been putting forward by way of interpreting (not explaining) social life in Herodian and post-Herodian Palestine.

Some indebtedness is long-term, like the debts of peasant communities; other indebtedness is relatively short-term, as in the world of those who are intent on commercial exchange, making money, and winning friends or influencing people. How debts are imagined depends on how completely a society is able to distinguish itself from the world of nature; how they are discharged depends on distinctions that societies can draw in separating specific social acts from individuals and their actions. Debts of obedience to rulers and of faithfulness to a divine covenant can also be imagined and discharged in ways that depend on how complex and well developed are a society's institutions. Some will pay tithes and other taxes; the degree of separation from nature will be decisive in this regard. Some will give votive offerings and others mere votes; whether the relationships are long- or short-term will make the difference. Some debts will be discharged by sacrifice and others by penance, perhaps according to whether the debt is horizontal or vertical. This is not the place to develop a theory of evil and the nature of various kinds of indebtedness; I am simply pointing out that social life is based on a wide range of debts under varying social conditions, the non-payment of which opens the door to the presence and effects of evil.

We will need another concept, however, to help us to conceive of what it is like to live in a world more – or less – permeated with evil. MacFarlane, speaking of peasant societies in general, notes that:

An archetypical example of such a world can be seen in much of continental Europe between the fifteenth and eighteenth centuries ... Throughout Catholic Europe the Holy Office of the Inquisition, in alliance with the state, set up an elaborate machine for seeking out and destroying secret evil . . . It is clear that, from rural peasant to Dominican inquisitor, few doubted the daily reality of Evil, the Evil One, and evil beings. (1985: 59)

It is such a world, I would suggest, that could be found in the first half of the first century in Palestine. It was a world of unpaid debts and of despair over losing access to the sources of life. To prevent the advent of a dreaded day of final payment, moreover, required extraordinary means of salvation. To conceptualize the demand for such a day and the dread it inspired, and to conceptualize also the belief in supernatural sources of life, it will be helpful to introduce the notion of *charisma*.

CHARISMA AND THE DEMAND FOR AN ACCOUNTING

Let us now return to our question concerning the ability of religion to alleviate the burden of despair and dread in the nation following the crisis of Herodian succession. First, in attempting to understand the eschatological fervor of the period, we may ask, "Why should there have been such a widespread demand for a final testing of grace and power?" The demand was so intense, in fact, that the followers of Jesus were instructed to pray for the opposite: for deliverance from the time of testing, the *peirasmos*. The same prayer asks for relief from all obligations: what is owed the self by others, and one's obligations to others. In the interaction between these two parts of the prayer, in fact, is one of our first hints as to the origins of eschatological fervor.

It is in the nature of charismatic authority to demand a test, a proving ground, not as an obligation or duty but as a right. It is the right of one who speaks with charismatic authority that his or her words should be fulfilled "in the hearing of them," so to speak; the charismatic word does not come back empty but closes the gap between language and reality. Charisma demands that others undertake new duties and obligations, and it is therefore also a source of heavy duty; nothing less than a total response will do. The charismatic authority claimed by warlords, brigands, and prophets was different only in the type of charisma claimed by the leader in question: charisma by military prowess, "booty" charisma, or the extraordinary grace and supernatural power claimed by the prophet.

Even – especially – Roman senators were charismatic figures, no matter how "sophisticated" Roman culture appears to be from the vantage-point of the twentieth century and in comparison with Palestinian Judaism of the Herodian period. Remember the comment of Paul Veyne quoted in the introduction, to the effect that a Roman senator "was not a man like other men. Whatever he said was public and was supposed to be believed" (Veyne 1987: 174). That is quintessentially charismatic authority. If Jesus also spoke with authority – not like the scribes and Pharisees – that type of speech put him in direct competition with the highest authorities of the Roman world. "Roman loyalty" also, Veyne reminds us, "was to a man, not to a pact" (1987: 175).

Charismatic authorities as unlike as the prophet and the Roman senator have in common the demand that they be tested. They "call for the question," as it were, that puts an end to discussion of relative merits and authority. Eschatological demand is therefore inevitable in a society where so much authority is based on charisma. A popular demand arises for a final test of competing claims to dominion, but it is a demand inherent in charismatic authority itself. Charisma is only fulfilled in being put to the test of others' response; it is justified only in struggle and victory, that is, in events that fulfill the meaning and confirm the truth of one's word.[2]

It may be difficult for citizens of a relatively "modern" world to grasp the intensity of this demand for proof in a culture that locates and concentrates charisma so definitely in specific heroes and institutions. In contemporary Western societies, charisma has become dispersed among a wide variety of individuals, each of whom is understood to be the bearer of a small measure of

---

[2] If this description of charisma seems to be informed by biblical narratives of Jesus (or, for that matter, of figures like Moses) seeking a following, consider this account of Roman piety: "The gods stood just above humans, so that it often makes sense to translate the Latin and Greek words for 'divine' as 'superhuman' . . . Given this conception of divinity, the Stoics and Epicureans were able to ask disciples to aspire to become sages, that is, mortal equals of the gods, 'supermen'" (Veyne 1987: 209).

divine right, even if that right be only to pursue life, liberty, and happiness. The transition from a cultic or political center into the mass of discrete individuals is what Shils (1975: 127ff.) has called the "dispersion" of charisma. Therefore one of the long-term effects of modernization has been to place every individual on continual trial in a never-ending process of probation and certification.

How is it, then, that charismatic demand for testing and certification leads to an expanding set of obligations and an increasing debt, as it were, to society? Just the opposite would seem to be the intention of charisma: that is, to declare that the individual or institution has a right to receive gifts, obedience, and sacrifice rather than to give them. Indeed, Weber makes it clear that charisma is quite demanding and requires obedience. It is a paradox, then, that charisma should result in its own subversion by adding to the burden of obligation.

Weber explores this paradox in some detail as it appears in a variety of charismatic religious styles. Take, for instance, his treatment of inner-worldly asceticism. On the one hand, he argues, the ascetic of this type claims a "unique religious charisma" (1922;1964: 167) and may therefore be in a state of mind approaching, but not quite reaching, self-deification. It is in the nature of the charismatic gift, however, that the individual cannot be quite sure; the problem is how to "become and remain certain of one's own state of grace" (1922;1964: 167). Therein lies the paradox, that the extraordinary individual should take on a wide range of mundane obligations to find the missing certification, when charisma is supposed to lift one beyond the mundane.

Weber resolves this paradox by arguing that charisma's conservative bias stems from the charismatic's own claims to transcendent authority. Those claims in the end legitimate the new status quo that arises from the charismatic followers' gains in the social order. More paradoxical is that charisma, despite its initial successes and promises to enhance the power of the followers of the endowed leader, tends to leave individuals in a state of helplessness as they wait for fresh infusions of divine grace: for parousias and apocalypses and the return of magical endowments. Further paradoxical still is that charismatic movements from the periphery tend to become consolidated in the hands of a new elite that discourages the claims of individual followers to charismatic authority; the new leadership thus seeks to make sure that whatever graces are claimed tend to edify the whole community rather than enhance the authority of the individual. It is the claim of the new leadership group, of course, that they – not the individual believer – have the interests of the whole community at heart. While I cannot pursue these several contradictions here, I would propose that the Jesus movement represents an attempt by Jesus to resist the attributions of charisma by his followers as well as to overcome the contradictions that accompany that attribution. I will return to this point briefly in the epilogue.

Because the gift is divine, one's field of testing is correspondingly global but not necessarily eschatological. Because charisma is supernatural, it calls for a high measure of self-restraint (asceticism), lest its powers, so to speak, be unleashed prematurely. Such nobility of spirit requires considerable humility, although as Weber quickly points out, this humility is of a very "dubious" nature (1922;1964: 174).[3] The charismatics who are unconvinced of their own extraordinary gifts and thus require testing will be unconvincing in their own display of ordinariness. The source of the gift being divine, and its scope universal, the recipients of such charisma are required to maintain what Weber calls an "alert, methodical control" of all aspects of their life; that is why the inner-worldly ascetic ends up in the paradoxical situation not of obligating others, but of being obligated. Thus Protestantism "taught the principle of the world as the sole method of proving religious merit" (1922;1964: 168).

That is why some Protestants weary rather quickly of a life-time of testing and look forward with varying degrees of

---

[3] Compare Veyne's comment about the Roman householder who would typically raise a toast to the emperor after dinner: "In drinking a toast to the emperor's sacred image after dinner, a man raised himself to the level of that ineffable otherness, proof of whose existence lay in the fact of its veneration" (1987: 214). This comment encompasses two of the characteristics of charisma noted by Weber: self-deification, and uncertainty that requires, therefore, constant testing.

anticipatory rapture to a final test of merit. Of course, not all forms of charisma enjoy quite the same paradoxical relation to the world; a gift that seeks to be imposing because it is divine need not embroil the individual in a hopelessly global and complex set of obligations. As the gift becomes more tenuous, the scope and intensity of obligations tend to diminish somewhat. In speaking of "contemplative mysticism," therefore, Weber notes that the self is more suffused with grace or reduced to being a mere vessel; grace becomes less of a permanent gift than a state of consciousness that can only be acquired with some discipline but never taken for granted. Obligations in the world are therefore to be avoided, although other individuals are encouraged to become obligated, if only to pay homage, to the "illuminati" (Weber 1922;1964: 169ff.). There is an "inconsistency" here, but not a paradox: that the mystic must depend on support from those who fulfill the very obligations that the mystic knows to be unconscionable and opposed to contemplation (Weber 1922;1964: 171). The "unilluminated" are essential to the mystic's attainment of a state of grace; others must pay by their immersion in the world for the mystic's freedom. Gandhi, it was once observed, was very expensive to those who sought to help him maintain his vows of poverty while traveling throughout India.

Midway between the paradoxical state of grace enjoyed, if that is the word, by the inner-worldly ascetic and the inconsistencies of the mystic are the inconsistencies of the "world-rejecting" ascetic. This type (according to Weber) constantly seeks to avoid or reconcile the contrary demands of generosity and violence, of life and the real world. The type relishes agonized appraisals of the relative merits and obligations of love and justice, since he or she can neither fully leave the world to its own devices through contemplation nor continually fulfill a wide range of obligations without becoming distracted from the struggle to protect, improve, and perfect the gift of grace itself (Weber 1922;1964: 169–170). The more that grace inheres in the self rather than in the world of people and things, the more the world is a problem. The more that grace can be tested through obedience, the more rigorous is the discipline and the more self-limiting is the life of the individual who is charismatically endowed. The more the gift itself is tenuous and the self capable of being perfected, the more contentious and contrary will be the pull of the world on the self. The more the self is emptied to receive charisma, finally, the more the world itself becomes empty of significance except as a potential source of support and adoration. The tension between self and world is most acute among those who, being in a position to impose obligations on others by virtue of their own charisma, seek to undertake a life of continual and perfect service. The tension is least acute and is reduced to a mere inconsistency among those who, in order to be worthy to receive the divine gift, place others in a position of obligation to support mystical endeavors. As the tension between the self and the world decreases, and as the requirement for testing becomes less continuous, the world becomes correspondingly less the scene in which the gifted will make their demand for a trial. In the case of the mystic, it is others who become obligated to pay. However, the more dispersed is the gift of grace, and the more widespread and continuous becomes the life of obligation, the higher will be the demand for an end: an end that is both a final test and a final relief from a life of obligation.

Even in the first century there were efforts to disperse charisma among wider segments of the population. The Essenes had associate members in the villages and towns who were under some measure of discipline and were obligated to support the community. Pharisees sought to extend the demands for purity, incumbent on those extraordinarily endowed, to wider sections of the population, although they typically made exemptions for the most mundane of occupations. The Romans themselves sought to expand the range of obligations in taxation, prayer, and sacrifice and, in so doing, to disperse the charisma of empire abroad. In expanding the range and weight of obligation, I will argue, the social systems of the first century added another level of demand for the eschaton: a demand for a relief from obligation, an end to payment and a final testing. As a defense against evil, therefore, charisma creates a whole new range of problems for a society to solve.

TESTING CHARISMA: SOCIAL DREAMS AND PILGRIMAGE

It is not only individuals but whole societies that have to cope with these paradoxes, contradictions, and inconsistencies. A society whose leadership is based on charisma of one sort or another will necessarily test its leaders often. Remember the first paradox, that is, that charismatic endowments require testing and recognition. Charisma in war or in the amassing of "booty" requires authentication before it can become authoritative: signs of healing, of prophecies coming true, and of a reversal of fortunes.[4] While individuals of faith and discipline can live a lifetime with such uncertainty, societies generally must seek and employ strategies to give a more limited play to charisma. As Turner (1979: 88) makes clear, ritual and, more generally, social dramas are the scenes in which this limited freedom is granted to the charismatic spirit.

Of the variety of social dramas that could illustrate this point, pilgrimage is perhaps the most pertinent to understanding the degrees of religious and political freedom claimed within first-century Palestine, at least prior to the fall of Jerusalem in CE 70. It was a major testing ground for individuals and groups seeking authentication of their spiritual gifts. Indeed, individuals who die on pilgrimage to Mecca are guaranteed beatitude, and those who complete that pilgrimage are guaranteed that they will be presented blameless on the day of judgment (Turner 1979: 121). It is possible, I am suggesting, that a similar anticipatory eschatology gave meaning to pilgrimages to Jerusalem.

On pilgrimage to Jerusalem, each step along the way derived meaning from the point of one's own origin and from the past of the nation; each step also anticipated the consummation that awaits the pilgrim not only in Jerusalem but at the eschaton. The apparent freedom and indeterminacy of the way opened up possibilities for fulfillment that would test, confirm, and

---

[4] For would-be emperors, there were other signs of authentication. For Tiberius these included a public procession, signs (quite literally "placards") of triumph over conquered peoples, other signs noting the laws he had passed, and perhaps oaths of allegiance: see Tacitus 1956;1988: 36.

enhance the charisma of the individual by linking personal merit with the national treasury of merit. Because of their departure from ordinary duties, individuals could walk through the fields as Jesus frequently did with his disciples (Luke 6: 1–6): behavior typical of pilgrims who are finding – and making – their own way (Turner 1979: 122). But their apparent freedom was usually contained within the parameters of the pilgrimage, whose destination was always the same. In this way the demand for testing and for the authentication of the individual's spiritual gifts could lead to a testing that, in the end, would add to the dignity of the cultic center and the nation itself. When pilgrimage fails, however, demand increases for a more radical attestation and a final testing of charismatic endowment: a final victory over evil itself.

I have been arguing that eschatological demand arises from the peculiarly intense interplay between charisma and its following. Charismatic leaders are tested in a variety of ways, whether by victory in battle, the fruitfulness of the field, or the fate of their followers. Uncertainty concerning the source and strength of the gift requires resolution. In societies where the charisma of leadership has not been made a matter of traditional, routine, or rational procedure, the more frequent and intense will be the demands for testing the gift of the spirit.[5] Secondly, the more charisma is tested in a wide range of social roles, statuses, and duties, the heavier will be the weight of obligation, and the more demand there will be for social dramas that provide simultaneously certification of the gift of the spirit along with release from ordinary obligations. As those social dramas fail to express and contain the tension that results from testing charisma in a wide range of social obligations, the demand for release may find political or even military rather

---

[5] Clearly this point applies to pre-70 Palestine, with its constant testing of leadership, rival claims to authority, prophetic challenges to the priesthood, and guerilla warfare. Roman society, however, was itself vulnerable to challenges from individuals and groups claiming charismatic endowments. Tacitus makes it clear that individuals claiming access to the fates through astrology, or public honors and triumphs for military success, or recognition for booty captured from the enemy were all rivals of the emperor, who accorded them honors with great care and no little suspicion (1956; 1988: 73, 90ff., 99, 103).

than dramatic or ritualized outlet. Finally, the dispersion of charisma into wider ranges of the population will add to the numbers of individuals seeking both testing and release, certification and freedom, consummation and free expression of their gifts. Pilgrimage, under certain conditions, may provide precisely such a popular dramatization of these demands. When other conditions permit, however, those demands may lead to innovation and insurrection, for example, to more direct, concrete, intense, and destructive forms of testing and release.[6] Crusades become a functional alternative to pilgrimage, since they, too, provide a release from daily duty, a testing of charisma, and access to the heavenly city. They are a functional alternative to pilgrimage, but not its equivalent, since one is far less likely to return from a crusade.

It is clear that in this analysis I have departed from Turner's analysis of pilgrimage. There are several reasons for this departure, and it may help to clarify them briefly here. The first is the rather static view of pilgrimage that stems from regarding it as an institutional "limen" (Turner 1974: 182–183): a protracted threshold within which a more difficult and enduring rite of passage occurs. Unfortunately, such an approach does not lend itself to explaining why pilgrimages turn into actual invasions of a city, or why sacrifices cease to be symbolic and become both real and bloody, like the disastrous Passover pilgrimage shortly after Herod's death. Turner's playful terminology adds to the difficulty of developing a more critical approach to pilgrimage when he suggests, for instance, that pilgrimage could be a "meta-structure" rather than an "anti-structure" (1974: 182). When is pilgrimage a metaphor for the more ordered and orderly world of duty and obligation? When is pilgrimage a powerful force in opposition to that world? When

---

[6] Even the Roman army could witness the transformation of an orderly group into a mob: Tacitus tells the story of a mutiny of three brigades of soldiers who demanded of Tiberius, soon after his succession (and therefore during a time of relative weakness), certain reforms in their pay, length of service, and rewards at separation; the soldiers lost their courage, however, when bad weather and a failing moon "seemed directly connected with their criminal actions"; afraid of "divine wrath," they returned quietly to less polluted quarters and waited for the verdict of Tiberius. Charisma is a fickle source of inspiration and authority, and the charisma of the people is easily subdued by the authority of officers and officials (Tacitus 1956;1988: 49–50).

does that opposition become direct, immediate, and violent? These are the questions to which Turner's analysis provides relatively little in the way of clues.

Possibly more useful, but still problematic, is Turner's reliance on the familiar dichotomies of status and contract. Turner uses these terms to describe different types of society and to distinguish traditional from relatively modern forms of obligation. The distinction is useful in explaining the difference between pilgrimages in the ancient or classical world of the Mediterranean and pilgrimages in more complex, contemporary societies: the latter kind of pilgrimage inevitably being more optional, voluntary, and more related to the interstices and gaps in the calendar and structure of modern societies than were pilgrimages in societies integrated by various forms of social standing. It is less likely for pilgrimages in the modern world, therefore, to present dramatic alternatives to the prevailing system or to make allegiances within that system more voluntary. The status–contract distinction is useful for suggesting that pilgrimage has become more tangential to prevailing orders.

As I noted in chapter 1, the pilgrim encountered increasing amounts of contract and exchange toward the end of the way; at the end, the more contractual aspects even of traditional societies exhibited their arrangements in the bazaar and fair bordering the sacred premises of the shrine (Turner 1974: 183). Turner (1974: 182) speaks in the same context of the paradox that pilgrims on the way to the most sacred shrine would encounter increasing signs of secularization. But to the devout Jew entering Jerusalem as a pilgrim at the Passover these contractual exercises would appear less as the secular than the profane; Jesus' cleansing of the Temple suggests that the precincts were polluted by the signs of contract, that is, the money-changers, who set the price to be paid for sacrifices offered by the pilgrims at major festivals.

There is another dichotomy used by Turner, one which is potentially more useful for understanding why the disruption of pilgrimages should add to the strength of demand for the eschaton. Turner (1974: 191) speaks of a "dichotomy" between shrines that are based on ancestry or political units and those based on fertility or deities of the earth. The former are exclusive and perhaps divisive, while the latter provide the base for a more widely shared set of beliefs and values which cut across political or other divisions. Within this division, Turner distinguishes centers for pilgrimage that are peripheral to major centers for political and economic activity from those shrines that are located in such centers. It would be possible to develop a typology of shrines and pilgrimages based on these two distinctions: Central shrines and peripheral ones would be two such types; ancestral and political, as compared with earth or fertility shrines, would be two more. Although such a study of what Turner (1979: 132) calls "pilgrimage *systems*" is beyond the scope of our discussion, it is important to note that the symbols of the imperial cult, transported from the center at Rome to Jerusalem, focused and intensified the conflict between early Judaism and the empire by closing the symbolic distance between the ancestral or political shrines of the Roman center and the Mediterranean periphery. The conflict came to a head at major festivals, especially during the crisis of the Herodian succession.

More to the point in this analysis is Turner's attempt to define the difference between pilgrimage in salvation religions and the initiation rites of tribal societies. The difference between the two forms of testing charisma is important for understanding the reservoirs of eschatological demand in the first century. In pilgrimage, it is the way itself that offers the opportunity both to acquire the coveted gift and to test one's gift. The way may be long or short; it may, as Turner suggests, never be completed; but it always provides a far more protracted and complex set of challenges, contingencies, and uncertainties than rites of passage:

Pilgrimage is part of a life-long drama of salvation or damnation, hinging on individual choice, which itself involves acceptance or rejection by an individual of "graces," or freely volunteered gifts, from God. Irrespective of one's intention, one is *changed* by initiation, *ex opere operato*. (Turner 1979: 129–130)

Pilgrimage, by protracting the test, allows it to reach a terminus which is less predetermined than that of a rite. Turner sees in pilgrimage the beginning of the modern world: linear instead of cyclical progression; optional instead of voluntary participation; contingent instead of determined progression from the beginning to the end; a matter of status either achieved or rejected rather than a matter of status imposed (Turner 1979: 128–133). Speaking of pilgrimages within Temple Judaism, he notes that they combined elements of inevitability and obligatoriness with a wide range of contingencies and exceptions (1979: 129).

What is clearly a foretaste of the modern world, then, is the extension of probation over a longer period in time and over far more space: an early acting out of the tendency to turn the life of faith into a lifetime of continual testing. Indeed, the rigors of the way provide the very tests that charisma seeks. Paul, for instance, is claiming that his charisma has been similarly tested in the trials of the pilgrim: for example, through the beatings, robbings, fatigue, hunger, and shipwreck that were the frequent lot of the pilgrim. The point is that, in this protracted form of testing, the end is both sought for and yet just out of reach. To protract and delay the time of testing, early Christianity may have turned pilgrimage into a way of life. Not only a functional alternative to pilgrimage that ends in disaster, Christianity may have sought a way that postpones the very trial in which it claims preliminary victory.

CHAPTER 6

The making of a theory

It is the task of the observer, I have suggested, to come up with a theory. Remember, of course, that this is an introduction to sociological method: not a book on theory itself. Our method here will therefore be necessarily inductive. That is, it will have to be developed from observations and insights, from assumptions and analyses rather than from a body of theory itself from which we might derive some working explanations about the crisis in the Herodian succession and its implications for Jewish Christian origins.

Let us begin with assumptions. In discussing recent collections of essays by social anthropologists I tried to describe two dilemmas that result in a double-bind within certain patrilineal traditional societies. On the one hand, these societies must gain access to the sources of life: women, children, the fields, ancestral spirits, and the vitality that is passed from one generation to the next. On the other hand, however, to lay hold of these sources of life is to recognize that one must eventually give them up. To gain life, then, it is necessary to offer sacrifices. That is the first dilemma. The second dilemma is like the first: its inverse, as it were. To ward off the threat of death, either directly or indirectly, traditional societies have sought to impose rules and rites for purification. That is, to keep at a safe distance from disruptive influences that might disturb a society's continuity and ability to reproduce itself, a society seeks to impose rules for purity. To observe these rules, however, it is also necessary to accept a circumscribed and diminished freedom of movement and association, for example, between men and women, the healthy and the sick, the young and the old, insiders and outsiders. To maintain this distance and to give up these freedoms, therefore, it is necessary to offer sacrifices. In this way desire is transformed into duty, public purposes are served along with private satisfactions, and societies reproduce themselves in miniature associations.[1]

Sacrifices, then, perform a double duty. On the one hand, they enable the individual or community to consume to their souls' satisfaction while yet displaying self-restraint; portions are reserved for the cult and the gods. On the other hand, individuals thus participate in the purification of the self and the community from the threat of decay and death; to avoid such pollution it is necessary for the individual to offer a sacrifice of the heart and the soul as well as of the body. To express and to fulfill these twin duties, then, various societies have developed sacrifices, for example, Passover and Pentecost, in which the community gathers to affirm its right to the sources of life and to ensure its distance from the sources of death and pollution. This is not the place to discuss these rituals in detail; I am merely seeking to stress at this point their hypothetical importance for the continuity of the nation. If the Passover and Pentecost were disrupted by riots after the death of Herod, their disruption reveals the depth of the succession-crisis in Israel at the time immediately prior to the period of Jewish Christian origins.

An adequate theory would therefore explain the causes of the succession-crisis and interpret what made the crisis itself such a serious event in the life of the nation. Interpretation, as I have suggested, combines an understanding of how various aspects of a system are interrelated, even when they may not appear to be so, with an understanding of what it is like to live under such conditions. With such an interpretation in hand, of course, one can go on to ask of New Testament scholars a wide range of questions about the possible impact of this succession-crisis on

---

[1] There is nothing remarkable about this way of formulating the dilemma or double-bind, i.e. between warding off death and acquiring satisfactions through a diminished form of sociability that reproduces the larger society. Veyne (1987: 190–191) notes that confraternities and collegia in antiquity not only provided their members with many satisfactions in eating and drinking that were glossed by civic duty and consummated in sacrifice to one god or another; they were also "make-believe cities" or "mimicked the political organization of cities."

the religious movements of the period. The movements might then be understood and interpreted as responses to the seriousness of the crisis; they might also be explained as attempts to address the causes of that crisis. The better the theory, the better will be the questions that it raises.

Finally, with such a theory in hand, one can begin the work of developing alternative theories out of the repertoire of sociology, social anthropology, and psychoanalysis: a deductive process that provides antidotes, or alternative theories, to ensure that one does not begin to work in a circular fashion out of a single theory that has been developed pragmatically from a mixture of assumptions, insights, and observations. To develop this alternative theoretical framework clearly will require a separate undertaking; here it is enough to show how a relatively simple theory could be developed out of Josephus' description of the succession-crisis and from our reflections on it.

In this study I have been looking at a single event and its immediate ramifications. It may be helpful, however, to set that event in a larger context, since it is indeed a prelude not only to the religious movements at the time of Jesus but also to the disastrous civil war of 66–73/4, which left an indelible mark on both the fledgling Christian community and on Judaism itself. It is to sketch in the larger dimensions of this period, then, that I begin with these reflections on the disputes over claims to entitlements or "social credit" that followed the highly contested and tumultuous succession of Archelaus to the throne of Herod.

Before going further, however, let me briefly cover some familiar territory once again, even at the risk of some repetition. In this book I am focusing on one set of problems: on how societies reproduce themselves. In the process of societal self-reproduction, I have suggested, it is necessary to do more than to transform desire into duty, although such a transformation is a prerequisite if societies are indeed going to reproduce themselves. It is necessary for individuals to replace others in a wide range of roles, especially in roles of leadership and authority. To do so it may also be necessary for individuals to be willing to sacrifice: to delay their entrance into these roles, to postpone indefinitely their rights of succession, and yet to keep hope for such entitlements alive.

This dilemma, that is – simultaneously limiting desires and satisfying them – leads at least patriarchal societies into various ways of symbolizing, and triumphing over, various symbolic and actual sources of opposition: women, unbridled sexuality, free-thinking individuals, innovations, outside influences, pollution, and death itself. Societies seek to embody these contradictions within themselves in order to triumph over them: to reveal within themselves the sources of life and defenses against death; all sources of negation are thus driven outside the symbolic – and sometimes the real – walls of the city. That is how evil is personified and triumphed over: by nominating a poor, disheveled creature to bear the brunt of a community's illusions about itself.

These symbolic triumphs are especially important when it comes to managing the succession of the generations, since the young may not be so easily co-opted, delayed, subordinated, and transformed into replicas of the generation that they are succeeding, just as the older generation may not be willing to pass on its entitlements to the young in due time. Under these conditions, the young develop closed networks: associations that do not replicate the larger society but in fact invert or subvert the social order. Fears of treason and sedition multiply, as do attempts by the older generation through spies and informers to pry open the secrets of these closed networks. Social appearances become increasingly deceptive; public performances become ever more adept, self-conscious, and subversive. These are some of the conditions, then, that make it exceedingly difficult for a society to reproduce itself. When these conditions are present, fears mount that time is indeed running out on the social order. That is, eschatological and apocalyptic speculations become increasingly intense and pervasive, as the society both fears and desires a final test of its powers over evil.

The appeal to charismatic sources of authority is always a source of instability in any society; hence it was important in antiquity for the political and cultural center to provide monarchical, priestly, or imperial models of stable spiritual endowment and supernatural authority to cow the periphery into awe if not into total submission.[2] None the less, charisma is evanescent, unstable, and – in modern parlance – "destabilizing" of the social order for several reasons. Weber pointed out, for instance, that charismatic leaders are sufficiently unsure of themselves to require constant proof and testing of their capacities to heal the sick, bring home booty, or win wars; their followers also require such constant proofs of their leaders' authority. Even more unsettling, however, is the long-term tendency of charismatic authority to compound duties even while claiming to free the individual from certain traditional obligations. These new duties, the unfolding discipline of the new order, as it were, may well require higher levels of sacrifice than the relatively routine sacrifices imposed by the old order. Indeed, the new duties may not only be burdensome but indefinite; it may be exceedingly difficult to know when one has done enough, as it were, in the service of a new mission under the authority of a new charismatic leader. This increasingly burdensome form of discipline also increases the demand for a final accounting and settling of debts: old debts and new ones. As a cure for the weight of traditional obligations, then, charismatic authority is also a new form of the same disease that transforms desires for life into life-constricting debts and obligations. This internal contradiction, I have argued, underlines the dynamic push in charismatic movements toward a final day of testing, when old debts will be satisfied once and for all.[3] Debt that is due

---

[2] The Roman order under the emperors was no less unstable because charisma was institutionalized in the emperor himself. These words by Seneca indicate the potential fragility of that order: The emperor "is the bond by which the commonwealth is united, the breath of life which these many thousands draw, who in their own strength would only be a burden to themselves and the prey of others if the great mind of the empire should be withdrawn . . . Such a calamity would be the destruction of the Roman peace, such a calamity will force the fortune of a mighty people to its downfall. Just so long will the people be free from that danger as it shall know *how to submit to the rein*; but if ever it shall tear away the rein, or shall not suffer it to be replaced if shaken loose by some mishap, then this unity and this fabric of mightiest empire will fly into many parts" (Seneca, *On Clemency* 1.4.1–2, quoted in Starr 1982: 52 [my italics]).

[3] Even Seneca has Nero saying, "Today, if the immortal gods should require a reckoning of me, I am ready to give full tale of the human race" (*On Clemency* 1.1.2–4, quoted in Starr 1982: 51). The reckoning is all the more drastic because the powers attributed by Seneca to the emperor are virtually total in their control over the life and death not only of individuals but of entire cities, peoples, and nations.

to a community's illusions about its charismatic potential must be paid off over and over again. Evil, after all, is the presence of unsatisfied debt in a community and must be expunged if the community is to be able to believe in its extraordinary endowment.

Now, in this chapter I wish to put some more detail on the picture of a society which is in fact undergoing such demands for relief from duties and for a settling of debts and accounts. Any society, I would argue, tries to create a surplus of wealth and of other, less tangible forms of honor, trust, loyalty, and unquestioned authority. To draw on that surplus is therefore risky, like a run on the banks that accompanies a financial panic. Such a run leads to a day of testing and final accounting: a day in which scores are settled and individuals declare themselves free of their obligations. On such a day, as it were, a society becomes bankrupt: literally unable to elicit the sacrifices that will enable it to reproduce itself in the future. The death of the social order becomes a very distinct possibility at such a grievous time: evil appears to have won the day.

THE ENDURING CRISIS AFTER THE DEATH OF HEROD

Palestine during the first century was in a crisis that eventually destroyed Jerusalem and the society of which Jerusalem was the moral, religious, and political center. To grasp the nature of that crisis, it may help to think of an acute shortage of "social credit." Such credit resides in a wide range of social institutions, from the financial and political to the religious and cultural. Sometimes such credit is concentrated in relatively few institutions, as in first-century Palestine. The Temple itself concentrated all these forms of credit from the financial to the religious, but it failed to exercise a monopoly. Instead of venturing a definition of social credit at this point, however, I would prefer to illustrate the notion of a shortage of social credit from what we can learn from Josephus about first-century Palestine.

Certainly the most obvious aspect of the shortage was financial. Debt was burdensome; indeed, we are told that throughout the Greek world social protest usually took the form of demanding "the abolition of debt" (Rajak 1983: 139). After the death of Herod the Great, crowds petitioned his successor, Archelaus, for relief from taxes, and during the siege of Jerusalem the Zealots destroyed the archives in which money-lenders kept their records (Rajak 1983: 118). The debt crisis not only affected politics and the economy but spilled over into religion, and during famines the country priests suffered severely because the high priests continued to demand various sorts of tithes.

Ishamael ben Phiabi's high priesthood was the first of two occasions when humble country priests allegedly perished from starvation because members of the high priesthood forcibly seized their tithes from the threshing floors. (Rajak 1983: 125)

Josephus records two famines in which similar suffering was inflicted on country priests by the higher functionaries: both of these in the decades between the death of Christ and the fall of Jerusalem. None the less, as a late indication that the weight of financial debt was borne as heavily by the religious as by the general population, the record is an important one. Financial debt in taxes, loans, and tithes was a major and cruel source of oppressive obligation in Palestine, and that burden eventually became overwhelming.[4]

By social obligation I mean simply *the cost of maintaining relationships*. Taxes are the costs of maintaining political relation-ships, just as tithes are some of the costs of maintaining relationships with the cultic center, while the payment of debts is the cost of maintaining relationships with the sources of financial credit, that is, money-lenders. In Palestine, those relationships were increasingly oppressive because of the domi-nation of the local economy by colonial rule. It appears that small landholdings were being aggregated into larger holdings, tenant farmers were being required to produce cash crops like olive oil for export, and wealth was therefore being concentrated in the hands of a few large landholders and in the commercial

---

[4] Palestine, of course, was not alone. Starr reminds us that "By and large revolt in the Empire was the product of overly heavy taxation or its unjust collection; newly added tribes on the frontier often can be found rising in rebellion one generation after receiving the blessings of Roman rule – and taxation" (1982: 78).

towns that provided access to distant markets (Rajak 1983: 119–120, 123–124). It was therefore not unusual to find families being sold into slavery for the payment of debt (Rajak 1983: 119). There was no doubt that the Romans did provide occasional protection from robbers or from murderous crowds, but the costs of security eventually outweighed its benefits as the countryside became increasingly dangerous and as gentiles, even those employed by Roman soldiers, became a source of danger. The costs of producing for a foreign market also increased when basic needs were not satisfied, expecially during famine; then even the priests starved as their tithes were extorted from them by the high priests of good family and advantageous position. Clearly, however, the purpose of all such taxation was to maintain the Roman aristocracy, with its system of masters and slaves; there was no escape from the economic consequences of this costly domination.[5]

Eventually the advantages of protection by the Romans, of export, and of cultic authority were outweighed by the costs, and freedom became the highest value of all. That is why the Zealots introduced new coinage during their occupation of Jerusalem; during the second and third years of the revolution their coins bore the inscription, "the freedom of Zion," and in the end spoke of the "redemption" of Zion, as if, its debts paid, Zion were freed from slavery to the Greco-Roman world, its markets, and its powerful political and military domination (Rajak 1983: 142). The same metaphor of redemption was also used by early Christians to express their liberation from all forms of indebtedness.[6]

---

[5] Tiberius is reported to have explained it in rather bald terms to the Roman senate thus: "without provincial resources to support master and slave, and supplement our agriculture, our woods and country-houses could not feed us. That, senators, is the emperor's anxiety. Its neglect would mean national ruin. For other troubles, the remedy lies with the individual. If we are decent, we shall behave well – the rich when they are surfeited, the poor because they have to" (Tacitus 1956;1988: 145).

[6] In this book I cannot begin to give an adequate social history even of the debt-revolts of that period. It may help to note, however, that the rebels in Jerusalem were not the only ones to seek relief from debt and sanctuary from the punishments of Roman law by taking refuge in various temples. Tacitus' description of revolts in previous decades, especially circa 22 CE, is telling: "In Greek cities criminals were increasingly escaping punishment owing to over-lavish rights of sanctuary. Delinquent slaves filled temples.

This crisis in social credit undermined the trust that individuals and groups placed in their leaders. Take Josephus, for example. He was a notable, a person of high social status who had links with the military and administrative officials of the Roman regime. Like many notables in the American colonies, he was expected to serve in various capacities and was eventually called upon to quell a revolt in the region of Galilee, where he served to no one's particular satisfaction and was eventually – but unsuccessfully – recalled from his duties for a variety of alleged failures, faults, and even betrayals of his country's cause. This is not the point at which to investigate the charges against him. My purpose is simply to point out that the crisis in the succession to Herod cast all forms of authority and leadership into question; the vacuum of responsibility was not easily filled. I am suggesting also that the religious movements of the period between the death of Herod and the civil war were repeated and unsuccessful efforts to fill that vacuum.

The treasury of merit, as it were, from which leaders draw their supply of social credit is the repository of many assets. Some of these assets are clearly utilitarian. Even charismatic leaders, for instance, require success in healing if they are to keep up the faith of their followers, and political leaders require fresh supplies of military victories or demonstrable success in preventing domestic disorder if they are to remain in their positions. These, I argued in the last chapter, are some of the burdens and obligations of charisma: escape from normal duties imposes higher obligations to demonstrate one's supernatural sources of power and authority. One failure can be fatal to charismatic authority; it is so evanescent. That is why I earlier referred to these sources of acclamation as the soft currency of legitimate authority.

Other assets, although less tangible, I have called the hard currency of legitimacy because they belong to virtues that reside within the culture: in a leader's lineage or household, for

Asylum was granted indiscriminately – to debtors escaping their creditors, even to men suspected of capital offences. Protecting religious observance, these communities were protecting crime itself; and interventions provoked outbreaks which no authority could control" (1956;1988: 148).

instance, as in the case of high priests who, as political leaders, received credit for their line of descent from families who had led prior revolts. The Hasmonean lineage is one example, and the house of David another. Other forms of credit were more abstract and derived from traditions coded in the Law; even country priests were worthy of a limited tithe, and the higher priests were entitled to more generous commitments from the populace, all on the basis of their standing within the Law of Moses itself. Social credit could be derived either from being a custodian of the culture or from conforming to it; those who managed to fulfill the requirements of purity were entitled to a certain degree of honor from those whose poverty or occupation prevented them from displaying such virtues. These forms of display were clearly under attack among several religious movements of the first century, however, and the Jesus movement is only one of the more celebrated forms of social protest against this form of social credit.

I am arguing that a vicious circle was in operation following the death of Herod; it made both purity more desirable and pollution more impervious to the solutions of ritual. As famine and contact with death became more widespread and inevitable, the anxious demand for an uncontaminated food supply and for avoiding pollution would intensify. Under these conditions, however, even scrupulous observance of the Law would not prevent either starvation or disease, and both war and famine could make observance itself either impractical or impossible. In the end, during the siege of Jerusalem, all forms of observance ceased, and bodies were dumped over the walls or allowed to accumulate unburied in the city itself. Where purity had had its staunchest defense, pollution was in the end most appalling. The early Christian community found other ways, therefore, of lifting the obligations imposed by the Law and of assuaging anxiety over death while still claiming to be able to accomplish the spiritual survival and symbolic reproduction of the nation of Israel.

In the mean time, however, social credit earned from the observance of the Law's requirements for purity was diminishing rapidly, and the demand for protecting the hard assets of the faith became more violent and intense. The Zealots' insistence on the strict observance of the Law and on the purity of the Temple itself was really an effort to preserve those few remaining, tangible as well as symbolic, forms of credit on which the whole society, its basic authority, was believed to rest. Zealotry was a form of fundamentalism that sought to prevent the bankruptcy of the system as a whole; it ended in the system's devastation, as the Zealots' sense of their own entitlements knew no bounds.

It was crucial that the vacuum left by the destruction of the Temple be filled, and early Christianity can be seen as one movement to supply an alternative sense of where the Temple is located, that is, among the body of believers. In that community of believers new forms of purity could be established that would no longer be rooted in the hard assets, so to speak, of cultic observance or of the Law. Purity and fidelity would find other forms of observance less vulnerable to social disorganization and to the anxiety of death itself.

A number of obligations were therefore put to the test in the siege of Jerusalem. One of those obligations comes from the division of a society into classes of notables, artisans, peasants, and landless workers. Noblesse oblige puts it exactly: nobility carries with it a number of obligations. These are the costs of maintaining the division of classes, and some of those costs were borne by the nobility themselves. Josephus, indeed, has argued that a "noble death" in battle against the Romans was preferable to captivity, but it was a sentiment that he attributed to a high priest; given the opportunity for a noble death, of course, Josephus chose survival and collaborated with the Romans.

The Jewish nobility were often suspected of such collaboration during the campaign conducted by Josephus in Galilee. Josephus was only one of several Jewish notables who were pressed into the leadership of the Jewish revolt despite their close ties to Roman officials and their own preferences for peace; their obligations, however, were to defend the Jewish community as well as to keep order: a quasi-feudal obligation to the artisans, farmers, and tradespeople who in turn conferred on them a range of entitlements. For instance, Ananus, a high priest who was one of the "reluctant revolutionaries," was pressed into

military command; Josephus records that Ananus did not
expect victory, but wished to enable the Jews to give "a good
account of themselves": a wish that, as Rajak seems to suggest,
could be interpreted as a plan to put up a mere show of fighting
(Rajak 1983: 130–131). Under these conditions, the costs of
maintaining noble status are minimized, while the lower strata
are required to bear the costs of defeat, further repression, and
continued sacrifice. It is understandable that the Zealots
massacred the notables and put an end to their own share of the
costs of maintaining others' dignity and status (Rajak 1983:
130). The early Christian community continued the resistance
to the entitlements of noble status and their attendant costs and
obligations.

TRYING TO UNDERSTAND WHAT IT WAS LIKE TO LIVE IN SUCH A CRISIS

In Josephus' *Jewish War*, there is an extraordinarily revealing
description of an encounter between Pilate and a crowd of Jews
who were protesting the presence of Caesar's ensigns in the
sacred city of Jerusalem. The sheer presence of the ensigns had
polluted the purity of that city, but it is the potency of the images
that is central in Josephus' account. It is as if the full force of the
Roman power and authority were contained in those images:
the power to create a people and to destroy them. To a modern
anthropologist, however, panic at the intrusion of such images
can be understood as stemming from a magical view of
authority, from fear of pollution, and from a strong desire to
sacrifice in order to guarantee that collective life will continue.

Mosaic Law prohibited images of any sort in sacred precincts.
Underlying that prohibition, I suggest, was the notion that the
image enjoys the potency of what it represents. Such a notion is
not entirely strange to Christians brought up in a sacramental,
liturgical tradition: there the potent symbol does convey what it
represents, i.e. the body or blood of Christ. The point is that the
prohibition of images in Judaic thought functions as a prohibition of magic itself. Unfortunately, however, like any prohibition, the injunction does not root out either the desire for power
or magical thinking.

Magic is often counterphobic; that is, it protects us from the very symbols and images that are the most frightening. That is precisely why the Law of Moses was itself considered to be the source of such purity and power that it could be offended only at the risk of death. Note, for instance, that Josephus (*Jewish War* II.8) is able to say that blasphemy even against Moses was a capital offense. Anyone who endangers the sources of magical power threatens the very life of the community; capital punishment simply fits the crime.

Unraveling the scene one thread at a time, then, makes it possible first of all to disentangle the strands of magical thought. Magical thinking is based on the most profound wishes and anxieties: the wish for life and the anxiety over helplessness, isolation, and the fear of death. Remember for the moment that magical thinking originates in that infantile mental state in which the child does not distinguish between the operations of the mind and the existence or processes of the external world. Others seem responsible for making the child think, feel, or indeed even exist in a certain way; conversely, the child seems able through speech or imagination to conjure up the presence of those on whom the child's life itself seemingly depends. No wonder that images, including Caesar's ensigns, seemed to have had such expressive significance, since they signified the people's own dreams of power and glory. It is also no wonder that those images seemed so fraught with danger in the possession of one who, like Caesar, indeed had the power of life and death.

It is not entirely foreign even to contemporary societies to find political figures invested, as it were, with such awesome powers. I mean this not only in the literal sense of the right to administer capital punishment or to save a society from mortal danger, but in the more abstract and yet vital sense of personifying and guaranteeing the life of the nation itself. Ernest Becker (1975;1976: 68–69), who relies heavily on the psychoanalytic understanding of magical thinking, also finds a central symbol for the society itself in the ensigns of a Caesar:

The emperors and kings who proclaimed themselves divine did not do so out of mere megalomania, but out of a real need for a unification of experience, a simplification of it, and a rooting of it in a secure source of power. The leader, like the people, senses a need for a strongly focused

moral unity of the sprawling and now senseless diversity of the
kingdom, and he tries to embody it in his own person:

> By proclaiming themselves gods of empire, Sargon and Rameses
> wished to realize in their own persons that mystic or religious unity
> which once constituted the strength of the clan, which still
> maintained the unity of the kingdom, and which could alone form
> the tie between all the peoples of an empire. Alexander the Great,
> the Ptolemies, and the Caesars, will, in their turn, impose upon their
> subjects the worship of the sovereign, not so much out of vanity as to
> consolidate moral unity . . . *And so through its mystic principle the clan has
> survived in the empire.* (A. Moret and G. Davy, *From Clan to Empire*,
> New York: Knopf, p. 360)

Perhaps Caesar's representatives were surprised, like Pilate,
by the people's superstitions; they may indeed have been seeking
to unify rather than divide a province of the empire by bringing
the image of Caesar to the sacred city of the Jews. I rather doubt,
however, that Pilate was surprised: after all, it was only a few
years earlier that rebels had torn the imperial eagle from the
Temple in Jerusalem. The point is simply that the supply of
social credit depended on a reservoir of magical thinking about
power and its symbols, a reservoir that could quickly run dry in
times of adversity. The Jesus movement may well have been a
response to just such an exhaustion of the treasury of social
merit. *Therefore, when social credit is exhausted, strong demand rises for
words that are as good as deeds. This "charismatic demand" seeks to close
the gap between language and reality for all eternity, as it were.*

When the symbols of Caesar, like the eagle over the Temple or
the ensigns in Jerusalem, penetrate the sacred precincts, Israel's
victory over death itself is threatened with defeat; the eagle was
a dangerous form of pollution in the body politic. Becker is right
that the stakes are very high indeed; collective and individual
immortality hang together. Outside the sacred community
there is no victory over death. The symbols of Caesar promised a
different transcendence over death, but they required the
surrender of Israel's own promise of victory over death: a
triumph that neither history nor nature should take away.
Diminish that victory, question that promise, and one might as
well destroy the treasures of the Temple itself. That is why the
crowd would have preferred to sacrifice their lives to Pilate

collectively rather than withdraw their demand that his ensigns be removed from Jerusalem. To conquer death, one must sacrifice life. In turn, such sacrifices add to the treasury of social merit on which a wide range of authorities can draw. That is a vicious circle indeed.

The practice of sacrifice is inspired by the attempt to lay hold of the sources of life, while making a promise to give it back at the end. It is as if life demands a *quid pro quo*, a death for every life that is taken; therefore sacrifice is necessary for that logic to be satisfied. Becker (1975;1976: 100ff.) indeed points out that sacrifice has many layers of meaning and cannot easily be captured in a brief synopsis. One sacrifices because one is humbled by the majesty of the natural and social world, and not only to achieve the purity and constraints that will ward off the threat of death itself. Sacrifice does embrace *an effort to overcome despair (over losing the sources of life) and dread (of death itself) by performing various symbolic operations on the world. Each operation includes the utterance of powerful speech; sometimes that utterance claims to be the saving event itself.*

When words fail, other tests are required to divine whether an enemy's magic is greater than one's own. Massive anxiety about collective power can sometimes be assuaged only by mass sacrifice. Becker, referring to Huizinga, reminds us that

war was a test of the will of the gods, to see if they favored you; it forced a revelation of destiny and so it was a holy cause and a sacred duty, a kind of divination. Whatever the outcome was, it was a decision of holy validity – the highest kind of judgment man can get – and it was in *his* hands to be able to force it. (1975;1976: 105)

The demand for a judgment, a trial by battle or by sacrifice, made the first century extraordinarily bloody indeed. Josephus' history of *The Jewish War* gives an overwhelming account of death: carnage, piracy, massacres, and the wholesale crucifixion or burning of insurgents. To understand the social context of the New Testament and the early Christian community without coming to grips with such terror and suffering opens the way to a grievous misunderstanding of the world in which Jews and the Jewish Christians of the period were living.

EXPLAINING THE CRISIS OF SUCCESSION

In Josephus' account of the events following the death of Herod, we noted the juxtaposition of two major festivals: the one sponsored by the state to manage the succession from Herod to Archelaus, the other a feast of the people at the time of the Passover. Their juxtaposition helped to account for the concentration and intensity of the conflict. At the Passover, collective memories of oppression in Egypt and of providential liberation may have reinforced popular demands for rescue from an oppressive Roman regime. There were two separate social systems at work here, and when they were juxtaposed with one another, the grief and the grievances generated through the rites of succession simply intensified the memories of past oppression and liberation that were enshrined in the rites of the people. While conflict was intensified by the juxtaposition of the two rites, their separation made that conflict exceedingly difficult to resolve.

The presence of these two systems within the same territory intensified without resolving the vicious circle which I described earlier. As I mentioned in the discussion of the New Guinea Highlanders, exchange with foreigners may be necessary to the survival of a community, although such exchanges may appear to certain communities as dangerous sources of pollution and as threats, therefore, to the community's ability to reproduce itself. In a society like Israel, dominated and partially penetrated by a colonial power, the people were required to have transactions with the enemy in order to survive; even in taking part in the rites of succession one guaranteed the continuity of the kingship and its vitality, at the cost of accepting some taxation or other forms of oppression. On the other hand, participating in the enemy's social system is a source of impurity and contamination; to participate requires that one run the risk even of rejection by one's own people for seeking favors from the world of a gentile oppressor. The subsequent revolt of the Passover pilgrims may have been one way of removing the impurity incurred by participating in the rites of Roman succession. It is necessary to reassert one's purity when one has come too close to the source of pollution and of death itself. That was why the crowd demanded a priest of greater "piety and purity" than the one who had been contaminated by guilty association with Herod. The revolt was also inspired by a desire for relief from taxes and imprisonment, that is, for lesser sacrifices.

When grief becomes politicized, ritual will fail to prevent more widespread and bloody sacrifices from taking place. It is difficult, of course, to imagine a nation as complex as the United States gathering in a cultic center to offer sacrifices in lieu of further bloodshed. It is also difficult to imagine that such a rite would be the delicate, last line of defense against the passions aroused by death. The rites of succession and of the Passover sought to express and thereby to contain the mixture of passions aroused in the hearts of survivors; and both failed in their respective function. Josephus' account narrates with some astonishment that the crowd went smoothly from stoning a tribune to observe their rites, apparently without any sense of guilt. The point, however, was not lost on Archelaus: the contagion of grief had spread too far for any rite to contain it; Josephus speaks of "disease" spreading to the multitude much in the way a modern social scientist would speak of hysterical contagion. When rituals fail and grief becomes politicized on such a scale, it requires an army to restore oppression.

In a sense, the slaughter at the Passover was a dress rehearsal for the failure of another ritual that followed fifty days later, that is, Pentecost. Josephus' entry is telling:

So, on the arrival of Pentecost . . . it was not the customary ritual so much as indignation which drew the people in crowds to the capital. A countless multitude flocked in from Galilee, from Idumaea, from Jericho, and from Peraea beyond the Jordan, but it was the native population of Judaea itself which, both in numbers and in ardour, was pre-eminent . . . Thus investing the Romans on all sides, they held them under siege. (*Jewish Wars* II.3.1; Josephus 1927: 339)

When a crowd gathers at the time and place of an especially important ritual, and the gathering also has been politicized, that ritual will fail and will continue to release powerful passions into the body politic rather than contain them within the bounds of the rite itself. Popular "indignation" is then beyond the capacity of the ritual itself to express, sublimate, and transform into the passions of a public and politicized grief. *Under these conditions, demands intensify for charismatic leaders whose words will elicit the sacrifices and create the symbolic victories over death that ritual fails to provide.*

Of course, it is not only in rituals that one perceives the juxtaposition of the two systems, Jewish and Roman: there are many ways in which these two systems could meet, overlap, or conflict rather than merely coincide. I am hypothesizing that there was a dialectic between the system of the Romans and the tribal organization of the Jews and that this dynamic interplay made it impossible for either system to guarantee either access to life or victory over death in their respective rites, rules, and social institutions.

Consider the interim period between the death of Herod the King and the crowning of Herod's successor. Josephus' account begins in Palestine and extends to a gathering of Jews and Roman officials before Caesar in Rome itself to determine the Palestinian succession. Note particularly the importance of crowds, "multitudes," and fighting units; note also the importance of what anthropologists sometimes call "big men": that is, military or charismatic leaders who often bring innovations or tip the balance in the conflict between a colonial power and a tribal society. The arrival in Jerusalem of crowds, still indignant, during Pentecost (*Jewish War* II.3.2), along with the presence of militant leaders, initiated a conflict not only in Jerusalem but over the entire countryside. An initial battle at the cloisters of the Temple caused high casualties on both sides, a fire in the works surrounding the Temple, and the plundering of the Temple itself. The fighting increased as more men, "in far greater strength and efficiency" (Josephus, *Jewish War* II.3.4; Josephus 1927: 343) arrived in Jerusalem to surround and besiege the Romans. Mercenaries left the king's party to join the Jews; others "go over to the Romans." The countryside erupted as various leaders commanded fighting groups: one was "the arch-robber Hezekias"; another "big man" was a servant of the king who plundered the palace at Jericho; a third was a shepherd with charismatic qualities who "had the temerity to aspire to the throne. He was called Athrongaeaus, and his sole recommendations, to raise such hopes, were vigour of body, a soul contemptuous of death, and four brothers resembling himself" (*Jewish War* II.3.3; Josephus 1927: 347).

Some villages were plundered and burned because they sided with the Herodians while others were burned by the Romans in revenge (*Jewish War* II.5). The social "order," as Josephus describes it, depended on strong ethnic loyalties attached to particular places and leaders rather than on more abstract and flexible loyalties. It was indeed an "order" quite familiar to students of religious and political movements in tribal societies that have been mobilized by their contact with colonial powers. Here it is important simply to see the social order of the period not only in the powerful loyalties to the cultic center in Jerusalem but also in powerful local ties and in allegiances to charismatic leaders who, by virtue of their appearance, fearlessness, or associations, commanded a following. It is in this complex, volatile, and incandescent mixture of political and religious gases, as it were, that one can begin to understand the conflagrations in the countryside and in Jerusalem.

INDICATIONS OF A CRISIS IN SOCIAL CREDIT: THE DEMAND FOR PAYMENT

It is questionable whether the crowd or their leaders knew the possible consequences of their opposition to Archelaus. In the parallel account that Josephus gives in his *Jewish Antiquities*, he is at some pains to infer that the Jews could be forgiven because they did not know what they were dong:

Meanwhile some of the Jews who had come together in their desire for revolutionary action began to utter lamentations for Matthias and his followers who had been put to death by Herod but because of the fear inspired by him had at that time been deprived of the honour of being mourned . . . They regarded as lawful and just whatever might be likely to give them pleasure, and they did not have sense enough to foresee any danger that might result therefrom. (*Antiquities* XVII.9.1,2; Josephus 1969: 467, 469, 471)

This disclaimer, however, is not very convincing. Josephus has already mentioned that the people were out for revenge against Herod for having killed those who had pulled down the eagle from the Temple; thus he adds:

> or if it ([danger] was to some extent suspected to exist, it was outweighed by the immediate pleasure that was expected by them from taking vengeance on those whom they most hated. (*Antiquities* XVII.9.2; Josephus 1969: 471)

The people did not merely demand that respect should be given where it had been denied. Those deprived of respect in life should receive it in death. What was operating here was a desire for revenge: the *lex talionis*, in the people's attempt to reverse their fortunes and to turn the tables on the gentiles and "king"; these were seditious as well as vengeful crowds, as Josephus notes of their "desires," their "designs," and their "wills." The people could hardly be unwitting of the dangers in which they were placed by their plans for "revenge."

There is no doubt, even in Josephus' mind, that the crowd may well have been aware that their revolt could be fatal in its consequences. Indeed, it is their demand for payment for past injuries that appears to Josephus as collective pathology: an evil victory over the forces of evil. If the presence of evil in a community is signified by a widespread and chronic sense that old debts have not been satisfied, the demand for a payment of such debts may seem to be an effort to overcome evil. For Josephus, however, such demands could lead to a far worse evil of public insurrection: a holocaust, as Cornfeld puts it in writing of the civil war in 66–73/4 CE. I regard it as an early warning of the eschatological demand for a final accounting. In that sense the Jesus movement, I would suggest, was one of several responses to that demand, the origins of which can be found in the succession-crisis that eventually culminated in the civil war of 66–70 CE. Demands for such a final accounting inevitably produce a "run" on the treasury of social credit, as priests and politicians are faced with a massive withdrawal of credit from the "church" and "state."

LIVING BETWEEN THE TIMES

The release of these insurgent, unpredictable, and passionate forces was not accidental, of course; it occurred in the protracted interval between the death of a king and the crowning of his successor: an interval marked by the public mourning for Herod and the mourning of the Jews "on their own account," as Josephus put it. The interval extended further during the period between the Passover and Pentecost: a period in which unsatisfied grievances and political prisoners now released could again raise hopes for the restoration of the kingdom. As Josephus noted of the crowd besieging the garrison left in Jerusalem after Archelaus had departed for Rome, they demanded that no one "stand in the way of men who after such a lapse of time were on the road to recovering their national independence" (*Jewish War* II.3.4; Josephus 1927: 343). Theirs was a hope that flourishes, so to speak, between the times: the hope, that is, that a society will be able to reproduce itself spiritually and historically despite the succession of many generations in which a former social order has in fact been realized at best only in fantasy and pious expectation.

When grief is politicized, the only possible redress is a drastic change in political conditions; however, when two systems are juxtaposed, as I have suggested, there is no single liturgical solution that will be effective in both systems at once. Take, for example, Josephus's account (*Jewish War* II.6) of what was happening in Rome precisely at the time that Jerusalem and the neighboring provinces were in revolt during the interregnum. Archelaus is in Rome to be named king by Caesar; his detractors among the Herodians as well as his political rivals are present at the hearing. Consider how the hearing before Caesar provides, as it were, a mirror-image or parallel of the constituencies in Jerusalem. There is a "crowd," as Josephus again points out, of Jews: fifty [*sic*] delegates from Jerusalem, supported by many of the Jewish community of eight thousand present in Rome; these stand in accusation of Archelaus and of his dead father, Herod. Instead of an unruly crowd, an orderly multitude, to use Josephus' term, stand before Caesar in an array not unlike the gathering of the people imagined in the apocalypses of the period. Instead of the Temple, however, in Jerusalem, the array is gathered in the Temple of Apollo at Caesar's palace; instead of the throne of heavenly grace, the throne is Caesar's. The scene no doubt made an impression on the apocalyptic imagination as a forerunner of the last judgment. Certainly, as Theissen (1977;1978: 74) points out, Jesus was well aware of the delegation sent from Jerusalem to prevent Archelaus' succession. As I have argued in earlier chapters, in Josephus' ideology the court of Caesar represents the providential seat of transcendent justice. The further removed from Rome is the trial, and the more Caesar is represented by surrogates and inferiors, the less serene is the republic and the more easily corrupted is the trial itself.

How could this scene have affected the Jesus movement's conception of their encounter with Roman authority? How could this sequence of events have affected the early Christian community's understanding of Jesus' trial and crucifixion, and of Pentecost itself as the period of a new succession to the kingship of Israel? How stimulating to the Christian imagination was this symmetry between the actors and institutions gathered in Rome, on the one hand, and in Jerusalem and environs on the other? The symmetry is not accidental; although it reflects Josephus' own ordering of the narrative, it is based, I have suggested, on the actual juxtaposition of the Roman and Jewish social systems.

Indeed, as the Jewish delegation pointed out to Caesar, the brief period of Archelaus' succession had already added to their list of grievances. In the following passage, Josephus summarizes the indictment of Archelaus and Herod placed before Caesar by these delegates:

The plaintiffs, being given permission to state their case, began by enumerating Herod's enormities. "It was not a king," they said, "whom they had had to tolerate, but the most cruel tyrant that ever existed. Numerous had been his victims, but the survivors had suffered so much that they envied the dead. For he had tortured not only the persons of his subjects, but also their cities; and while he crippled the towns in his own dominion, he embellished those of other nations, lavishing the lifeblood of Judaea on foreign communities. In place of their ancient prosperity and ancestral laws, he had sunk the nation to poverty and the last degree of iniquity. In short, the miseries which Herod in the course of a few years had inflicted on the Jews surpassed all that their forefathers had suffered during all the time since they left Babylon to return to their country in the time of Xerxes. And yet so chastened and habituated to misfortune had they become, that they had consented to this bitter servitude being made hereditary and had actually chosen the heir themselves!" (*Jewish War* II.6.2; Josephus 1927: 355)

The crowds that provoked Roman aggression were in fact demonstrating that an entire social order was at stake. The crowd dramatized what the delegates later expressed in an articulate plea before Caesar, that a society was perishing, no matter how many individuals might live or die.

SUMMARY

The first century in Palestine pitted two sacrificial systems against each other. The ensigns of the Romans promised immortality to the faithful and threatened the remainder with summary proceedings or bloody reprisals. The Temple and the Law promised a victory over death that could be achieved only through sacrifice: sacrifice at the Temple, the giving of tithes, the purification of one's daily life, and finally – if necessary – the immolation of the body by fire or the sword. Ernest Becker captures some of this ethos in his own description of the human struggle to overcome death through trial, battle, purge, and sacrifice; all wars, he argues, are "holy" in that they can be seen as

a revelation of fate, a testing of divine favor, *and* as a means of purging evil from the world at the same time. (1975;1976: 115)

The violence that drove Jews and Romans to victimize each other was a result of intense demands for control over the sources of life and an acute anxiety over death: an anxiety that was heightened by the very violence to which it gave rise. That is the vicious circle that Becker speaks about; there is literally no end to a cycle in which one people gains its symbolic victories over death by exploiting and – in the last resort – killing another people. Despite his lack of enthusiasm for Becker's version of this vicious circle, Lifton himself offers a remarkably similar description in his treatment of "victimization":

Victimization involves the creation of a death-tainted group (of victims) against which others (victimizers) can contrast their own claim to immortality. Victimizers actually experience a threat to the life of their own group, around which they justify their actions. There are innumerable ways in which that sense of threat can be displaced onto those selected as victims. But once that has been done, a lasting target has been found for the victimizing imperative. (1979: 302)

It would be difficult not to see the Jews as a lasting target for the Romans' claim to immortality, and it is apparent that the Romans provided the crucial threat to the Jewish national claim to a symbolic victory over death. Their competing claims called for a final test, in which God was their judge, their witness, and their source of final vindication as well as rescue. That test came in the final siege of Jerusalem, and Josephus' account leaves no doubt that the stakes in that horrifying contest were terrifyingly high. *Under these conditions, deeds have replaced words, and silence reigns.* Is it not possible that the Jesus movement was an effort to prevent that final test, to fill the vacuum of authority created by the crisis of succession, and to fill the treasury of social merit by once again linking words to deeds? This marriage of language to reality, the incarnate logos, was an alternative to demands for a final test of claims of access to life and of national victories over death. When that marriage fails, there are no alternatives to a final accounting. That, at least, is the beginning of a theory. It will take an entirely separate work to provide the theoretical alternatives which can set the terms for a more vigorous sociological inquiry into Palestinian society and Jewish Christian origins.

As I argued in chapter 1, the succession in a patrilineal society must go smoothly if that society is to continue to believe in its ability to own and control the sources of life. If life is indeed to go on, sons must succeed fathers, and kings-designate must succeed the former ruler, if the society in question is going to reproduce itself. That process of reproduction occurs in many spheres: in the fertility of the fields, in the deference of the young to the old, in success in hunting or in agriculture, in mining or in manufacture, in the martial or in the fine arts. The issue in each case is the same, that is, that the vitality of the society depends on the succession of one generation and of one regime to another. A society whose vitality is in question leads its members into a sense of despair: a haunting and increasingly palpable suspicion that the promises of future and abundant life will never be realized.

More is at stake in the process of succession than a society's capacity to feel alive and confident of its ability to reproduce itself. The threat of death must also be laid to rest. That threat does not come, as I argued in the introduction, only from the more obvious and literal dangers posed by enemies, animals, illness, and domestic violence. The threat of death also comes from the real and symbolic sources of opposition to the structure of the society itself. You will remember that in a patriarchal society, women and sexuality are two such sources of opposition. In a society closed to outsiders, intermarriage with women of other communities, like exchange with outsiders, poses a very real threat to the society itself. The more the society relies on strict controls of individual behavior, the more it will see in sexuality and in individuality sources of opposition that threaten the community with the death of its controls and traditions. Societies that are unable to ward off such threats from various sources of opposition tend to inspire a sense of dread: fear and suspicion that an evil will come which will in fact put an end to the social world as people know it.

Epilogue

In order to reproduce itself any society must ensure that the next generation knows the language of the community and, more than its language, the rules for engaging in the most fundamental aspects of speech. At its core, I have suggested, a society consists of acts of speech such as appeals and confessions, lies and testimonies, conversations and addresses, exhortations and demands, questions and laments. When a society cannot be sure how to "take" someone, that person becomes suspect. When that person is someone in authority, the very credibility and the legitimacy of a society are at stake.

Now, there are many reasons why a society's acts of speech should be difficult to construe. In this short methodological essay I have pointed to a few of the factors that make language and speech even more than usually suspect and slippery. When generations are in subtle conflict, when the dependent generation both idealizes but also envies the older generation and its powers, then the stage is set for speech to be slippery or even deceptive. When, moreover, one generation reveals itself only in networks that are closed to the older one, speech itself becomes not only oily but opaque. In addition, both generations may inhabit two social systems that interpenetrate and rival each other, so that it is seldom clear in what capacity a particular individual is speaking or even to what audience. Under these conditions, I have argued, the stage is set for social dramas like rituals or trials to reveal the true meanings of speakers' words and their real rather than their stated intentions. Under these same conditions, moreover, when these rituals and trials fail to provide the requisite revelation, demands mount for dramas

182

that will reveal – once and for all – the motives and the intentions of all whose speech has been suspect. At those times it is essential to speak quickly, to the point, and to let one's "yea" be "yea" and one's "nay" be "nay."

To put it simply, I have been suggesting that in Herod's reign and demise we can find the reasons why the nation could not reproduce itself from one generation to the next. Those reasons have to do partly with the rivalry of sons with fathers and of brothers with each other. That rivalry, however, was both the result and the cause of a widening gap between language and reality, between what was said and what was either meant or actually done, and between public appearance and personal character. In turn, the breach between language and reality made it virtually impossible for the nation to construe individual actions, whether of sedition or compassion, into acts of treason or sacrifice.

To misconstrue actions was more than Herod's private misfortune; it is potentially disastrous for a nation to be unable to construe actions into acts. The repertoire of acts is the nation's infrastructure, as it were: the underlying structure that must be renewed and reaffirmed if the nation is to be able to survive and renew itself. That is why solemn rites provide just that sort of occasion in which actions are construed into acts, once and for all, when the last word is spoken and all is both said and done. Only a nation that can thus conduct its public discourse can establish a public truth that can be acclaimed. In the absence of such a public order, the pressure on Israel's rites to close the gap between language and reality was even more intense: a pressure that rites such as those at the Passover or Pentecost could hardly withstand or satisfy.

Even in the twentieth century one can observe regimes that are analogous in this respect to the Herodian kingship. Lincoln (1989) has noted that in Swaziland the king's enthronement takes place in the Ncwala ritual: a ceremony designed to force brothers to bury their rivalry and swear oaths of loyalty to the new king. The ceremony seldom succeeds, however, in purifying the kingdom of the brothers' rivalry, and each Swazi king therefore lives in fear of his brothers' plots and reprisals. Treason is a continual source of pollution in the body politic. Recently a trial for treason occupied the attention of the Swazi kingdom; the alleged plotter was a half-brother of the king who had been passed over by the queen mother when she nominated the current king to the succession. Rumors, allegations, sorcery, witchcraft, and the continual fear of both the king's supporters and his enemies for their lives typifies that regime, as it also characterized Herod's, and that for quite similar structural reasons.

In this book, however, I have been focusing on the further possibility that the presence of an age-set, a younger generation of males, was structurally responsible for much of the dissension not only in Herod's household but in the nation itself. Certainly the rivalries between Antipater, Alexander, and Aristobulus were intense enough to undermine Herod's command of his own household and to threaten the succession with chaos; as I have noted, these fratricidal conflicts were not limited to that household but typical of mid-Eastern kingdoms in which rival brothers laid claim to their inheritance.

Furthermore, the young, male age-set would translate fraternal rivalries to the larger society, where they could unsettle not only families but groups and institutions; eventually they could undermine a regime with their demands to control the succession of the king of the Jews.[1] Herod himself had to watch his brother, Pheroras, very carefully. Once Herod demanded an oath of loyalty to himself and to the Roman emperor: a loyalty test to which the Pharisees and Essenes naturally objected. Although Herod therefore fined the Pharisees for their non-compliance, his sister-in-law (Pheroras' wife) immediately leapt to the Pharisees' aid and paid their fines for them: a clear sign of fraternal rivalry that could not have been lost on Herod the king or on the larger society.

None the less, these rivalries would only make the survival of any particular dynasty or regime precarious; they would not automatically threaten the ability of a nation to reproduce itself

---

[1] It is clear that the brothers Alexander and Aristobulus were very popular in the public's view, and that Antipater was widely hated. On the relevant intrigues in Herod's palace, see Cornfeld (1982: 110).

culturally and thus to ensure its continuity from one generation to the next. That is why I have focused on the substructure of Palestinian society: on the way that one generation is prepared to undertake the responsibilities of another, on the attendant rivalries and subterfuges of this process of succession, on the network of relationship within and between lines of descent, and on the way that solidarities of speech are formed that include some and exclude others, to the detriment of public discourse.

In this process a "legitimacy crisis" comes to mean something far more pervasive and critical than, for instance, a crisis in the authority of high priests or a general suspicion of rulers, Herodian or otherwise. The legitimacy crisis extends to all persons who lay claims to authority, and that includes the younger generation as it succeeds the older in positions of responsibility and trust, whether in occupations or the ownership of the family farm. When generations cannot succeed each other smoothly, of course, any society loses its ability to reproduce itself. What follows will not be an extension or fulfillment of the past regardless of the relative order or chaos of the new regime.

Even so, a crisis in the succession of the dynasty and in the survival of the nation as a unit would not have such far-reaching implications if the discourse of the society itself were not in peril. After all, Catalonia has survived as a province of Spain and has maintained a high degree of cultural integrity even if it has lacked autonomy. The same may well be said of the ethnic enclaves within Eastern European nations, and of nations like Latvia, Lithuania, or Estonia even while they have been made into provinces of the Soviet empire. What matters in the long run for societal reproduction, I have argued, is whether or not a particular society is able to establish the word: to make language a trustworthy vehicle for social exchange and the making of sacrifice. Agrippa may have had a point: that is, so long as the nation lacked autonomy and its own spiritual integrity, it had more intractable problems than the highly questionable wisdom, judgment, or effectiveness of the Herodians to whom were entrusted the fragments of Herod's kingdom after his death.

Now, in a later work on sociological theory and the study of

the New Testament, I will be able to show how the fledgling
theory that I have been developing in this essay could be refined
and challenged by a more systematic theoretical argument: one
which could yield a design for research into the social background of the Jesus movement and the earliest Jewish Christian
communities. In approaching the problem of societal reproduction from a Marxist viewpoint, for instance, I would investigate
the way in which the division of labor is determined by a
patriarchy, which also controls the distribution of the surplus of
production. How were men and women assigned to roles in the
economy, allowed to inherit land and other property, or given
access to the means of production and control over its surplus?
This approach raises a wide range of very thorny questions: for
instance, whether one can even use concepts such as class in the
first-century context.[2]

Our purpose, however, would be to investigate how the
producers, those who did the work, were engaged in the process
of reproducing the social system. Here again we would focus on
language. For instance, we could investigate how the process of
reproducing a society through forms of address was interrupted
by the Jesus movement. By refusing to honor people with titles,
the Jesus movement may well have been cutting at the tie that
binds individuals to a repressive social order. The withholding
of a title can indeed be an inflammatory act; it can also alter the
consciousness of the individual who refuses to speak in ways that
reaffirm the existing distribution of entitlements, honors, and
social distinctions.

On this basis I would propose, then, that a crisis of legitimacy
comes when a movement refuses to engage in the symbolic
reproduction of a society. That refusal, one could argue, is what
made the Jesus movement potentially revolutionary, but that is
a subject that can only be explored in the context of a theory that
provides alternative and conflicting propositions. Otherwise the
argument would be self-fulfilling and tautological.

---

[2] The Marxist viewpoint is represented by G. E. M. De Ste. Croix, *The Class Struggle in
the Ancient Greek World*, Ithaca, N.Y.: Cornell University Press, 1981. For what I would
consider to be a definitive treatment of the concept of classes and the question of
whether the social system of the ancient world in the first century was capitalist, see
W.G. Runciman, "Capitalism Without Classes," *British Journal of Sociology*, Vol. 34,
No. 2, June 1983: 157–81.

Other theoretical viewpoints lie close at hand, of course, in the work of Max Weber. His quasi-Marxist argument traces the symbolic disruption of a social order to the rise and fall of charisma: from charismatic movements among individuals and groups on the periphery to the embodiment of charisma in the cultural and political institutions of the center. In pre-70 CE Palestinian society, charisma was indeed institutionalized in the Temple cult, controlled by elite groups of families, and in intellectuals like the Pharisees. But charisma is hard to monopolize and often erupts far from the institutions of the center, for example, among extraordinary individuals who claim exemption from mundane duties and disdain the usual paths by which individuals succeed to positions of authority; the eruption of charismatic leadership and movements thus represents an immediate threat to the legitimacy of any social system and attacks the usual methods by which generations succeed one another. The fate of charisma, however, is to be expropriated by dominant groups, who then seek to restrict charisma to the political or cultural center. Its fate is to be conservative: a not surprising *denouement*, if one considers the conservatism implicit in the charismatic's appeal to supernatural sources of legitimation.

From a Weberian starting point, then, it would be possible to develop another set of propositions to guide research into the social context of the New Testament. For instance, one could argue that the crisis of legitimacy stemmed from the development of charismatic leaders and groups on the periphery who succeeded in rejecting the authority of the Temple. In the same way, one can trace the origin of the civil war to the refusal of a priestly group to offer prayers for the emperor: a clear attempt to withhold charisma from the Roman political center and to encapsulate it on the periphery of empire. We can also explore the question whether there is a connection between the heavy obligations imposed by charismatic leaders on their followers and the demand for a final accounting: a day of ultimate reckoning.

This last question directs our attention, first of all, to the dynamics of the Jesus movement. It is obvious that Jesus did seek to disengage producers, like fishermen, from their everyday duties in order to get them to undertake the new duties imposed by his mission; that is "par for the course" for charismatic movements. Otherwise his followers would have been in a double-bind; what they were doing as workers, in an oppressive system, would also serve to perpetuate that very system. It is a double-bind that women in modern societies, for instance, know all too well. To have a position in the division of labor that allows one only to reproduce the conditions of one's oppression is a form of slavery; it makes a mockery of any form of free speech. In fact, double-binds are characterized by language that often conceals its opposite meaning; "yes" really means "no," and an apparent rejection may also veil a hidden assent. It may well be that to break out of that double-bind requires a radical simplification of language: to let one's "yea" be "yea" and one's "nay" be "nay," as it were. On the strength of this suggestion one could also propose that some of the injunctions given by Jesus to his disciples were attempts to get them out of the double-bind that makes it necessary to reproduce an oppressive social system if one is to have any place at all in making things or in getting and spending.

However, the task of reproducing a society places a heavy responsibility on the shoulders of those who take it up: responsibility for the life and death of the society itself. Now, charisma does impose new and heavier duties on the followers of charismatic leaders; it does seek a testing of endowments on the field of historical battle, whether the weapons are spiritual, military, or economic. Did the Jesus movement seek to counteract this pressure for a day of reckoning? Did Jesus seek also to lighten the duties of his followers, for example, by suggesting that his "yoke" was "easy?" Did he also seek to neutralize attributions of charisma, by rejecting all charismatic titles and attributions? Can Jesus be considered a charismatic leader regardless of his self-understanding, since charisma is indeed attributed to a person regardless of his or her wishes? From the continued expectations of a parousia and the resulting longing for a day of testing, can we also infer that there was a certain passivity or helplessness among his followers after his death, as the effects of magic wear off without leaving residues of

competence and authority? Remember that the Roman senator, too, was a charismatic figure: not like "ordinary" men.
What the senator said was to be believed and acted upon. It may
well be that the social periphery of Palestinian Judaism was so
hungry for countervailing powers that it would have had to find
in Jesus the counterpart to Roman authority: a man whose
words were to be believed and fulfilled in obedient response,
wherever they led.

From still another theoretical starting point, however, one
could trace the legitimacy crisis, not to class-conflict, to tensions
between generations, or to opposition between charismatic
sources of inspiration and authority on the periphery and the
institutions of the center, but to what Durkheim would have
called "collective effervescence." From a Durkheimian viewpoint, indeed, collective effervescence is constitutive of traditional societies; it is the forge which shapes a bond between the
individual and the society as a whole; hence Durkheim's
fascination with aboriginal societies that turned the chaos of
annual orgies into the means by which individuals received and
renewed their individual identities as members of the clan. On
the other hand, such effervescence can be a threat to any social
order when it provides deviant sources of individual identity
and conflicts with central institutions. Pilgrimages, for instance,
can be the process by which crowds assemble, individuals
achieve maturity in the eyes of the community, and the center is
renewed by the devotion of the faithful from the periphery who
come literally from afar to make their gifts at the shrines of the
center. The same pilgrimages, as Josephus noted, can be the
sources of fatal disruption.

In the course of developing alternative theoretical viewpoints, then, I would also have to consider propositions
developed from a Durkheimian starting point. I would propose,
for instance, that crowds in the first century were pivotal
institutions both in the reproduction of the social system and in
its dissolution. Crowds would be the primary social context, for
instance, for understanding the origins of the Jesus movement
and the formation of the earliest Jewish Christian gatherings in
Jerusalem after his death. Most importantly, in crowds we may

discover the process by which a society, unsure of its own charismatic endowments and burdened with unsettled accounts and debts, develops pressure for a final accounting.

When movements of cultural and political defense cannot guarantee the reproduction of a society from one generation to the next, some will be tempted to risk the death of the entire society in order to guarantee its regeneration.[3] Some forms of rebellion, even in relatively advanced societies like the Judaism of Palestine in the first century prior to 70 CE, are thus "archaic" in the sense that they employ unrealistic, irrational, even magical means to defend and reproduce the society itself. It is as if the Zealots wished to fight fire with fire and pit Jewish strength against Roman might in combat that was more highly symbolic of Armageddon than conceived in the light of the best military information and strategy. Such contests have charismatic significance as tests of inspiration, authority, and cultural superiority in the face of evil and death. They have little to do with the pragmatic attempt to recover ownership and control over the worlds of work and politics. That is why such struggles seem inevitably to verge on madness and suicide: a point that Josephus seldom failed to make either in his own comments or in the speeches attributed to Agrippa, Titus, and Vespasian.

What would have been the fate of Israel had the king's household continued to embody the society with all its gaps and contradictions? Suppose an orderly succession had allowed Israel to preserve its identity, manage its relations to Rome, and keep an uneasy truce within its boundaries between Jew and gentile, Hasmonean and Herodian, Galilean and Judaean?

---

[3] Note, however, the struggle against Alexander Jannaeus because of his Hellenizing tendencies and his illegitimate usurpation of the role of high priest. The Jewish opposition stopped short of a victorious rebellion when it became clear that the victory, through an outside alliance, would cause the annexation of Israel to the Seleucid kingdom. Many Jews rejoined Alexander rather than risk the annexation of the kingdom by the rebels' ally, Demetrius; see Schürer–Vermes–Millar 1973, Vol. 1: 224. The willingness to risk destroying the nation in the name of purification from outside influences was not strong enough at that time to make this rebellion into a disastrous civil war that could end only in the defeat of the nation as a whole. Clearly the level of frustration and despair after the death of Herod and at the time of the civil war was considerably higher.

Obviously we cannot know the answers. The problem is that history provides no controlled experiments. There were no two Israels that were similar in all respects except one: the success or failure of the royal succession. Instead, I simply suggest that when the succession between regimes and generations fails, all the cracks in a system become overt contradictions; conflict, once sublimated in ritual, returns to the streets. When the rituals of a society can no longer buy time and postpone the day of reckoning, time quickens, and becomes scarce and vitally significant, filled with portents and fatal consequences.

References

Becker, Ernest. 1975. *Escape From Evil*. New York: The Free Press. Reprint, 1976.

Bloch, Maurice. 1982. "Death, Women, and Power," in Bloch and Parry 1982: 211–230.

Bloch, Maurice and Jonathan Parry (eds). 1982. *Death and the Regeneration of Life*. Cambridge: Cambridge University Press.

Braund, David. 1985. *Augustus to Nero: A Sourcebook on Roman History 31 BC–AD 68*. B & N Imports.

Burkert, Walter. 1979. *Structure and History in Greek Mythology and Ritual*. Berkeley: University of California Press.

1987. *Ancient Mystery Cults*. Cambridge, Mass.: Harvard University Press.

Charlesworth, James H. 1988. *Jesus within Judaism: New Light from Exciting Archaeological Discoveries*. New York: Doubleday Anchor.

Cohen, Shaye J. D. 1987. *From the Maccabees to the Mishnah*. Philadelphia: Westminster/John Knox.

Cornfeld, Gaalya, General Benjamin Mazar and Paul L. Maier (consulting editors). 1982. *Josephus: The Jewish War*. Grand Rapids, Mich.: Zondervan.

Eisenstadt, S. N. 1956. *From Generation to Generation: Age Groups and Social Structure*. Glencoe, Ill.: Free Press.

(ed.). 1967. *The Decline of Empires*. Englewood Cliffs, N.J.: Prentice-Hall.

Feldman, Louis H. 1984. *Josephus and Modern Scholarship (1937–1980)*. Berlin and New York: Walter de Gruyter.

Feldman, Louis H. and Gohei Hata (eds.). 1987. *Josephus, Judaism, and Christianity*. Detroit: Wayne State University Press.

1989. *Josephus, the Bible, and History*. Detroit: Wayne State University Press.

Geertz, Clifford. 1989. *Works and Lives: The Anthropologist as Author*. Stanford: Stanford University Press.

Goodman, Marvin. 1987. *The Ruling Class of Judaea: The Origins of the*

Jewish Revolt against Rome AD 66–70. Cambridge: Cambridge University Press.

Grant, Michael. 1973. *The Jews in the Roman World.* London: Weidenfeld & Nicolson.

Guhl, Ernest Kar and W. Koner. 1889. *The Life of the Greeks and Romans* Translated from the 3rd German edition by F. Hueffer. London: Chatto & Windus.

Gumperz, John J. (ed.). 1982. *Language and Social Identity.* Cambridge: Cambridge University Press.

Harris, Olivia. 1982. "The Dead and the Devils among the Bolivian Laymi," in Bloch and Parry 1982: 45–73.

Hengel, Martin. 1980. *Jews, Greeks and Barbarians: Aspects of the Hellenization of Judaism in the Pre-Christian Period.* Philadelphia: Fortress Press.

Josephus. 1927. With an English translation by H. St. J. Thackeray, MA, Vol. II, *The Jewish War*, Books I–III. London: William Heinemann, and New York: G. P. Putnam's Sons.

Josephus. 1969. With an English translation by Ralph Marcus, completed and edited by Allen Wikgren, Vol. VIII, *Jewish Antiquities*, Books XV–XVIII. Cambridge, Mass.: Harvard University Press, and London: William Heinemann.

Josephus. 1981. *Complete Works.* William Whiston, trans. Cedar Rapids, Mich.: Cedar Rapid Publications.

Jupp, T. C., Celia Roberts, and Jenny Cook-Gumperz. 1982. "Language and the Disadvantaged: The Hidden Process," in Gumperz 1982: 232–256.

Kee, Howard Clark. 1989. *Knowing the Truth: A Sociological Approach to New Testament Interpretation.* Minneapolis: Fortress Press.

Lifton, Robert J. 1979. *The Broken Connection: On Death and the Continuity of Life.* New York: Simon & Schuster.

Lincoln, Bruce, 1985. *Religion, Rebellion, and Revolution: An Interdisciplinary and Cross-Cultural Collection of Essays.* New York: St. Martin's Press.

1989. *Discourse and the Construction of Society: Comparative Studies of Myth, Ritual, and Classification.* Oxford: Oxford University Press.

MacFarlane, Alan. 1985. "The Root of All Evil," in Parkin 1985: 57–76.

MacMullen, Ramsey. 1974. *Roman Social Relations: 50 BC to AD 284.* New Haven and London: Yale University Press.

Middleton, John. 1982. "Lugbara Death," in Bloch and Parry 1982: 134–154.

Parkin, David (ed.). 1985. *The Anthropology of Evil.* Oxford: Basil Blackwell.

Perowne, Stewart. 1956. *The Life and Times of Herod the Great.* Sevenoaks: Hodder & Stoughton.

Rajak, Tessa. 1983. *The Historian and his Society.* Philadelphia: Fortress Press.

Runciman, W. G. 1983. *A Treatise on Social Theory,* Vol. I, *The Methodology of Social Theory.* Cambridge: Cambridge University Press.

1989. *A Treatise on Social Theory,* Vol. II, *Substantive Social Theory.* Cambridge: Cambridge University Press.

Samir al-Khalil. 1989. *Republic of Fear: The Inside Story of Saddam's Iraq.* New York: Pantheon Books.

Schürer, Emil, Geza Vermes, and Fergus Millar. 1973. *The History of the Jewish People in the Age of Jesus Christ (175 B.C.–A.D. 135),* a new English version revised and edited by Geza Vermes and Fergus Millar, Vol. I. Edinburgh: T & T. Clark.

Shils, Edward. 1975. *Center and Periphery: Essays in Macrosociology.* Chicago: University of Chicago Press.

Sievers, Joseph. 1989. "The Role of Women in the Hasmonean Dynasty," in Feldman and Hata 1989.

Stambaugh, R. and Balch, D. 1986. *The New Testament in its Social Environment.* Philadelphia: Westminster Press.

Starr, Chester G. 1982. *The Roman Empire 27 BC–AD 476: A Study in Survival.* Oxford: Oxford University Press.

Strathern, Andrew. 1982. "Witchcraft, Greed, Cannibalism, and Death, Some Related Themes from the New Guinea Highlands," in Bloch and Parry 1982: 111–133.

Tacitus, 1956. *The Annals of Imperial Rome.* Translated with an introduction by Michael Grant. Revised edition, Harmondsworth: Penguin, 1988.

Theissen, Gerd. 1977. *Sociology of Early Palestinian Christianity.* John Bowden, trans. Philadelphia: Fortress Press. 2nd edition, 1978.

Turner, Victor. 1969. *The Ritual Process.* Hawthorne, N.Y.: Aldine.

1979. *Process, Performance, and Pilgrimage: A Study in Comparative Symbology.* New Delhi: Concept.

1974. *Dramas, Fields, and Metaphors: Symbolic Action in Human Society.* Ithaca, N.Y.: Cornell University Press.

Villalba, I. Varneda, Pere. 1986. *The Historical Method of Flavius Josephus.* Leiden: E. J. Brill.

Veyne, Paul. 1987. "The Roman Empire," in Paul Veyne (ed.), *A History of Private Life: From Pagan Rome to Byzantium.* Cambridge and London: The Belknap Press of Harvard University Press: 5–234.

Weber, Max. 1922. *The Sociology of Religion.* Ephraim Fischoff, trans. Boston: Beacon Press; Beacon paperback, 1964.

Welker, Michael. 1989. "Righteousness and God's Righteousness." Paper presented at the Neumann Symposium, Princeton Theological Seminary.

Woodburn, James. 1982. "Social Dimensions of Death in Four African Hunting and Gathering Societies," in Bloch and Parry 1982: 187–210.

Young, Linda Wai Ling. 1982. "Inscrutability Revisited," in Gumperz 1982: 72–84.

Author index

al-Khalil Samir 91, 98

Balch, D. 83, 86
Becker, Ernest 169ff., 179ff.
Bellah, Robert 31
Berger, Peter 31, 84
Bloch, Maurice 34, 37, 40f., 44, 47ff., 78ff.
Braund, David 33, 74
Burkert, Walter 41, 112

Charlesworth, James H. 25, 26
Cohen, Shaye J. D. 14, 16
Cornfeld, Gaalya 17, 39f., 86f., 129, 176

Davy, G. 170
De Ste. Croix, G. E. M. 186
Douglas, Mary 26, 31
Durkheim, Emile 46, 81, 189

Eisenstadt, S. N. 20
Evans-Pritchard, E. E. 30

Feldman, Louis H. 14, 24
Freud, Sigmund 101, 141

Geertz, Clifford 31, 75
Goodman, Marvin 11, 16ff., 22
Grant, Michael 6, 7, 10
Gumperz, John J. 106

Harris, Olivia 46
Hata, Gohei 14
Hengel, Martin 10, 17f.
Huizinga, J. 171

Jones, A. H. M. 21
Jupp, T. C. 104—5

Kee, Howard Clark 28ff.
Klein, Melanie 101
Kreissig, Heinz 24

Lincoln, Bruce 183
Luhmann, Niklas 32

MacFarlane, Alan 139f., 144f.
MacMullen, Ramsey 106
Middleton, John 137f.
Millar, Fergus 15, 29, 41, 97f., 190
Moret, A. 170

Nikiprowetsky 39

Parkin, David 34, 37
Parry 34, 37, 40f., 43f.
Parsons, T. 32
Perowne, Stewart 6, 8ff., 15
Plutarch 11

Rajak, Tessa 163f., 168
Runciman, W. G. 61, 64, 68f., 73ff., 84, 91ff., 112–13, 116, 119, 121, 123, 126, 130, 186

Schurer, Emil 1, 5, 29, 41, 97f., 190
Shils, Edward 147
Sievers, Joseph 49
Stambaugh, R. 83, 86
Starr, Chester G. 161, 163
Strathern, Andrew 43f.

Tacitus 13, 94, 152f., 164
Theissen, Gerd 177
Turner, Victor 4, 27, 41, 135, 157ff.

Varneda, Pere Villalba I 13ff.

196

Vermes, Geza   1, 5, 29, 41, 97f., 190
Veyne, Paul   4, 72, 76

Weber, Max   43, 55, 69

Woodburn, James   50

Young, Linda Wai Ling   83

Subject index

Agrippa 185, 190
Alexander 10, 57, 62, 66f., 79, 86, 92,
    94ff., 99, 102ff., 107, 112, 116f., 123f.,
    184, 190
Alexander Jannaeus 10
Alexandra 9, 29
Ananus 168
Antigonus 95, 113
Antioch 92
Antiochus 10
Antipas 1, 41
Antipater 59, 63, 75, 79, 86, 91, 94ff.,
    100, 104, 113ff., 184
Antipatris 40
Antony 6
Arabs 6–7, 9, 37, 97, 105
Arabia 97
Archelaus 1, 17, 18, 51, 53, 57, 81, 92,
    94, 107, 129, 135, 163, 172, 177
Aristobulus 6, 9, 10, 57, 62, 86, 92, 94ff.,
    99, 102ff., 112, 116f., 123f., 184
Armageddon 190
Athrongaeaus 174–175
Augustus 10, 13, 39, 53f., 57f., 62, 65ff.,
    71ff., 81, 82, 92, 97, 114ff., 119ff.,
    129, 134, 169f., 174, 177ff.

Ba'athist Party 91, 98
Beijing 121ff.
Berenice 9

Caesarea 39, 102
Caligula 1
Catalonia, Spain 185
Chaerea 37
China 74
Christianity 33, 47, 156, 168
Claudius 37
Congress, United States 61

Cordus 12
Crete 80

David, King 36, 63, 166
Demetrius 190
Dung Gate 26

Edomites 6
Earls Colne 139f.
Essenes 26, 42, 150
Estonia 185
Etero 44f., 125
Eurycles 106–7

Gaius 37
Galileans 2, 9, 190
Galilee 1, 6, 25, 26, 132, 167, 173
Ghandi 149
Glaphyra 92

Herodias 1
Haight-Ashbury 138
Hasmoneans 6, 9, 17, 49, 166, 190
Henry VIII, King 9
Herodians 1, 177
Hitler, Adolf 134
Hussein, Saddam 98
Hyrcanus 6, 9

Idumaea 6, 173
Idumaeans 6, 9, 10
Iraq 91, 98
Ishamael bon Phiabi 163
Israel 5, 10ff., 15, 18, 39f., 48, 124, 130,
    132, 134, 190–1

Java 75
Jericho 173

Jerusalem   25, 26, 38–9, 42, 56, 62, 68, 151, 154, 167, 174, 177f.
Jesus   28, 38, 48, 60, 63, 65, 71, 145ff., 159, 188ff.
Joseph   63, 126
Judaea   6, 16, 17, 22

Latvia   36, 185
Laymi   46f.
Lithuania   185

Mariamme   9, 10, 37, 62, 68, 75
Mary   63, 126
Mattathias   6, 175
Melpa, New Guinea   43ff., 125, 172
Merina   48
Middle East   12
Moses   166, 169

Narbo   74
Nero   161
Nicolaus   57, 114ff.

Ottomans   11

Palestine   1, 10, 30, 33ff., 56, 71f., 117ff., 162ff.
Passover   24, 38, 135f., 153f., 158, 173, 177
Paul   60, 156
Pentecost   38, 158, 173, 177f.
Peraea   173
Phaedrus   12
Pharisees   29, 60, 141, 150
Pheroras   62, 95, 105, 184
Pilate   1, 132, 170
Protestants   148

Qumran   25

Romans   16, 17, 146, 150, 164ff, 174f., 178ff.
Romans, Epistle to the   60
Rome   10, 39, 118, 177–8
Russia   61–2

Sabinus   1, 37
St. Bartholomew's Massacre   9
Salome   9, 37, 62f., 68, 75, 92, 97, 105
Samaria   1
Saturninus   110
Sejanus   12
Seleucids   11, 190
Seneca   12, 161
Soviet Union   61, 185
Spain   183
Stalin, Joseph   98, 134
Swaziland   183
Sylleus   97, 105, 119

Tiananmen Square   74, 121ff.
Tiberias   41
Tiberius   12, 13, 153, 164
Tiro   98ff.
Titus   190
Torah   11, 20, 30, 44, 127

Varus   114–15, 117
Vespasian   190
Volumnius   110

Woodstock, New York   138

Zealots   164, 167f., 190

Index of biblical citations

Matthew
  10:17–19 89
  10:21 91
  10:25 102
  10:26–27 115
  10:28 96–7
  10:39 96

Mark
  3:31–35 63
  4:22ff. 49
  4:40–41 64
  5:1–20 49
  7:11 59
  9:29 64
  13:12 59
  14:36 59

Luke
  2:48–49 63
  4:21 64
  5:24 64
  6:1–6 152
  6:46–49 64
  7:8–9 64
  7:22 64
  7:30–50 141
  8:26–39 141
  9:60 36, 40
  11:28 64
  14:26 63
  15:11–32 63, 67, 71

Romans
  8:15 60

Deuteronomy
  21:18–22 103